Mary Gave God a Body

Mary Gave God a Body

PAUL O. BISCHOFF

RESOURCE *Publications* • Eugene, Oregon

MARY GAVE GOD A BODY

Copyright © 2018 Paul O. Bischoff. All rights reserved. Except for brief quotations in critical publications or reviews, no part of this book may be reproduced in any manner without prior written permission from the publisher. Write: Permissions, Wipf and Stock Publishers, 199 W. 8th Ave., Suite 3, Eugene, OR 97401.

Resource Publications
An Imprint of Wipf and Stock Publishers
199 W. 8th Ave., Suite 3
Eugene, OR 97401

www.wipfandstock.com

PAPERBACK ISBN: 978-1-5326-6270-6
HARDCOVER ISBN: 978-1-5326-6271-3
EBOOK ISBN: 978-1-5326-6272-0

Manufactured in the U.S.A.   10/31/18

For Melanie

Contents

Preface | ix
Introduction | xiii

Chapter 1
Obedient | 1

Chapter 2
Blessed | 9

Chapter 3
Ecstatic | 15

Chapter 4
Contemplative | 21

Chapter 5
Wondered | 27

Chapter Six
Conflicted | 33

Chapter 7
Frightened | 38

Chapter 8
Overwhelmed | 43

Chapter 9
Pushy | 49

Chapter 10
Insulted | 53

Chapter 11
Devastated | 58

Chapter 12
Restored | 63

Conclusion | 67

Bibliography | 75

Preface

THE SON OF GOD was an illegitimate child. Mary was his unwed teenage mother. Her future spouse Joseph was not her child's father. An angel told Mary that a holy spirit would mysteriously impregnate her. Mary had no idea how this would happen. At first she was upset. It would look like she lost her virginity. She'd appear to be an adulteress punishable by death according to Jewish law. But she agreed to allow this mystery to occur in her body. Joseph suspected that his wife-to-be was unfaithful and thought about divorcing her. An angel told him that no other man was involved and that he should just take her home as his wife. He did. Elizabeth, her cousin, was the first person Mary told about her conversation with Gabriel. Elizabeth had her own unique birth story and blessed Mary as the mother of her Lord. The initial events surrounding Jesus' birth were at best suspicious and at worst scandalous.

There was nothing religious about Jesus' birth. Only two unofficial godly people were actually waiting for the arrival of messiah. Simeon and Anna. Both were unofficial members of the temple. No official temple teachers or synagogue leaders showed up at the manger; only shepherds and astrologers. A jealous puppet leader, Herod, wanted to murder Mary's son. Innocent children under two years old were killed to make sure Mary's baby would be one of them. To escape, angel told Joseph to take his family to Egypt and then return to Nazareth, a small obscure village further north where Mary raised her family.

Preface

Mary was an unknown Mediterranean girl whose primary task in life was to save herself for marriage, tend the hearth and operate a loom. God favored her and chose her to conceive, bear, deliver, and raise the son of God. It was Mary who gave God what he needed to save humanity–a body. God could not have come to us as spirit, mind or soul. No one would have ever seen him. God needed a body to accomplish his mission. He arrived in human flesh. The Word became flesh. Mary's flesh.

Mary was created in the image of God and stained with original sin like any other human being. Historically, the church has not allowed Mary to be human amd denied her right to be a sinner. Mary has had to be perfect and pure. But her son only came to save sinners. Mary knew she was a humble sinner. She realized her place as a servant. She never claimed to be sinless, only blessed. The church has claimed more for Mary than she ever claimed for herself. Essentially, the church has romanticized, spiritualized and domesticated the mother of God. Current Christian traditions have either idolized or neglected Mary who predicted that future generations would call her blessed; that is, one empowered by the grace of God. Mary had nothing to do with saving the world beyond giving God the body he needed to live, suffer, die, and rise from the dead. Mary's son Jesus saved the world, not she. She'd quickly correct any attempt to call her co-redeemer. Mary would tell the church to pray to her son, not to her. She'd tell us to go through Jesus to get to the Father. Not to go through her to get to her son.

The purpose of *Mary Gave God a Body* is to portray Mary as an ordinary human being. She had the same weaknesses common to any human being. The biblical witness to Mary's sons verifies her interest in perpetuating humanity with no need to perpetuate her virginity. We surmise that she lived to at least forty-eight. She's last mentioned in Scripture at the beginning of the fledgling church spawned thirty three years after Jesus' birth. Mary simply took her rightful place as a parishioner in the early church with her sons by her side. There is no reason to doubt that Mary died a natural death; even if her bones have yet to be discovered. The assumption that Mary was translated from life to heaven has no biblical support.

Historic religious tradition has created a gnostic Mary; that is, one without a body with only a virtual existence. Mary will wear no haloes in this book. She'll wear no crown. That said, she'll be presented as the mother of God, the most unique mother on earth, who was favored by God. She brought Jesus up to be a son of the commandments as any Jewish mother would. She scolded him, challenged him and pondered the unique experiences she had raising this special child. It wasn't easy being God's mother. That bitter-sweet role confronted Mary with anxieties and frustrations throughout her life.

Mary Gave God a Body is based upon the premise that "good anthropology spawns good theology." You will be reading about the human Mary of the Bible. The book focuses upon Mary's encounters with Jesus from the canonical record written in the Gospels. Any analysis of Mary from oral tradition or historic church councils is mentioned only as the decisions from those sources have made their way into the Bible. All we need to know about Mary is documented in the Scriptures, the authoritative rule for faith and practice in the church. That said, extra-biblical suggestions, admittedly speculative, as to how Mary might have felt or behaved in her encounters with Jesus permeate the book. Such suggestions constitute historical fiction designed to make Mary real. *Mary Gave God a Body* proposes no "theology of Mary." Rather, it points out how Mary's life contributes to the incarnation, the doctrine about God's earthly embodiment. Any theology associated with Mary is in fact Christology about her son Jesus of Nazareth. Mary, we believe, would tell us that it's not about her, but Jesus. May your encounter of Jesus Christ as Savior and Lord be enriched by Mary's life as the first disciple of the church. Without Mary, the Word could not have become flesh. We would have never known the Jesus who her "adopted" son John wrote about as that one he "heard, saw and touched." May the intimacy Mary had with Jesus similarly encourage our faith in him.

Preface

Finally, an obvious disclaimer is required when a man writes a book about a woman. Especially about a mother, not to mention the mother of God. I'm fully aware of the risks involved. I recognize how identity theology has compartmentalized Christian theology into feminine theology, black theology, liberation theology and a host of other theologies. Each of these has its place. But all theology matters. Christian theology applies to all human beings, not particular segments of humanity. Human diversity allows for any segment of the human family to apply the rigor of theological analysis across the board. Her influence as the first disciple is not confined to women. Nor are only women qualified to write about her. Her doubts, questions, obedience and human authenticity minster across all boundaries be they gender, race or class. Clearly, Mary plays a unique role in the lives of any mother about which a man knows nothing. We male theologians have much to learn and unlearn from women about their historic reverence of Mary's son and contribution to the church and Christian theology. No woman abandoned Jesus at the cross. Men ran away for their lives. The only person who stayed at the cross to whom Jesus first appeared after coming back to life was Mary of Magdala, a faithful follower.

So I urge all Christians, Catholic, Orthodox and Protestant, to read this book with an open mind possibly learning again for the first time what it might mean to be a Jesus-follower from the blessed mother of God, the God-bearer, *theotokos*. On a personal note, my own faith has been encouraged by taking a human view of Mary as a disciple. I trust yours will as well.

My wife Jayne served as the primary source I needed to speak of Mary as a woman, wife and mother. I'm indebted to all those women whose contributions during seminars have seasoned many thoughts in this book.

January 1, 2019
Paul O. Bischoff
Feast of the Blessed Virgin Mary, *Theotokos*
Wheaton

Introduction

MARY OF NAZARETH IS the subject of this book. Her encounters with Jesus dominate how the Bible records her life. Her often-conflicted conversations with Jesus especially capture our interest. Jesus and Mary had a tense relationship. The chapter titles are named to reflect her various moods and emotions. Two types of interpretation of the biblical witness comprise each vignette in the Mary–Jesus dialogue: first, *fact* derived from the actual text and second, a subjective assessment of *feeling*. While most of this book is rooted in the inspired canonical accounts of Mary's life, some of it is historical fiction. We often pose the question: "How might Mary have felt in this situation?" The biblical text rarely gets into Mary's feelings stating only that she pondered and treasured things in her heart.

Your views of Mary may be challenged. If you're Catholic or Orthodox, you may see Mary as co-redeemer for salvation along with Jesus Christ or one to whom you pray. If you're Protestant you may have marginalized Mary as unimportant. You may have a difficult time saying, "Mary is the mother of God." If you are not religiously aligned, I encourage you to consider how you feel about God, Jesus, a Holy Spirit, the Bible and the church because we will discuss Mary in light of the above persons and concepts. This book is not a novel about Mary. Mary's story is important only as one told within God's story. We write it with the hope that it will draw you into a closer relationship with God just as she experienced. Mary's relationship with Jesus serves as a model. She

Introduction

is the supporting actress in the drama for saving humanity. Not to trivialize his life and ministry, we nominate Jesus for best actor–and he gets the Oscar.

Given anthropology's contribution to sound theology, our discussion of Mary's humanity is designed to enrich the reader's grasp of God. We offer a both-and approach of Mary as an ordinary human being and mother of God. Seeing her only through a religious lens tends to fog her humanity. Viewing Mary without faith reduces her story to a scandalous romance novel. Both views taken together are intended to characterize your reading. No chapter will get into technical theological concept or terminology. All theological interpretation is reserved for the Conclusion. There, at Dietrich Bonhoeffer's suggestion, we intend to voice theological concepts using non-religious language with a human dialect. Just as we hope to make a human Mary more accessible as a disciple, we also intend to convey the historic doctrines of the church without in-house jargon.

Structurally, this short book is divided into twelve brief chapters. Each is entitled with one word which conveys Mary's attitude, emotion or mood during a specific encounter with Jesus. A paraphrased biblical text from which the story is taken appears at the outset of each chapter. I encourage you to read it as background prior to getting into each vignette. I'm particularly indebted to Alfred Edersheim's *The Life and Ministry of Jesus the Messiah* as a resource for the cultural, historical, religious, social, and political background within which Mary lived. For the sake of uninterrupted readability, his and others' contributions do not appear as footnotes but are credited in the Bibliography. Our view of Mary's dynamic relationship with Jesus reaches its zenith at his birth. The events of her life up to that point are positive and encouraging. From the dedication to the cross, Mary's life is characterized primarily by tension, misunderstanding and conflict. Statements in quotes are Mary's unless explicitly attributed to someone else.

The Conclusion interprets Mary's life theologically. Unlike traditional conclusions, it not only summarizes the book, but also contains new information. Part of that new information is a brief

Introduction

analysis of the incarnation. A major teaching of the church. In the Conclusion we'll get into three theological concepts linked to the incarnation: grace, prophecy, and the church. We treat each of these as a summary of four chapters. Grace summarizes Mary's life up to and including Jesus' birth as discussed in chapters one through four. Prophecy is both proclaimed and fulfilled in chapters five through eight spanning the dedication through the Passover pilgrimage to Jerusalem. Finally, the definition of the church is anticipated and informed by the last events of Mary's life mentioned in chapters nine through twelve–from the wedding at Cana through her participation in the early church. The Conclusion ends with a brief analysis of the incarnation as the over-arching doctrine of Christianity from which all other church teachings derive.

The intent of this book is to state the ever-familiar stories of Jesus' life non-religiously. We propose a human Mary with no claim to exhaust telling the Jesus-Mary narratives non-religiously. The reader is encouraged to continue the process. Here's an example of the theological concept of obedience spoken in non-religious vernacular. It's a quote from Mary to the servants at the wedding in Cana. "Do what he says." May the church heed her advice. Who knows, a miracle might occur?

Chapter 1

Obedient

Luke 1: 26-38 and *Matthew 1: 18-25*

When Elizabeth was six months pregnant, God sent the angel Gabriel to Mary, a virgin pledged to be married to Joseph, a descendant of David. The angel said to her, "Greetings, one who is preferred by God! The Lord is with you." Mary was greatly troubled at his words and wondered what kind of greeting this might be. But the angel said, "Don't be afraid, Mary, God is pleased with you. You will be with child and give birth to a son, and you are to give him the name Jesus. He will be great and will be called the Son of the Most High. The Lord God will give him the throne of his father David, and he will reign over the house of David forever, his kingdom will never end." "How will this be," Mary asked, "since I am a virgin?" Gabriel answered, "The Holy Spirit will come upon you, and the power of the Most High will overshadow you. So the holy one to be born will be called the Son of God. Even Elizabeth in her old age, who had a hard time having a child, was now in her sixth month. For nothing is impossible with God." "I am the Lord's servant," Mary answered. "May it be to me as you have said." Then the angel left her.

Mary Gave God a Body

This is how the birth of Jesus Christ came about: His mother Mary was pledged to be married to Joseph, but before they came together, she was found to be with child by the Holy Spirit. Because Joseph her husband was a righteous man and did not want to expose her to public disgrace, he had in mind to divorce her. But after he had considered this, an angel of the Lord appeared to him in a dream and said, "Joseph son of David, do not be afraid to take Mary home as your wife, because what is conceived in her is from the Holy Spirit. She will give birth to a son, and you are to give him the name Jesus, because he will save his people from their sins." All this took place to fulfil what the Lord has said through the prophet, "The virgin will be with child and will give birth to a son, and call him Immanuel, which means, 'God with us.' " When Joseph woke up, he did what the angel of the Lord had commanded him and took Mary home as his wife. But he had no union with her until she gave birth to a son. And he gave him the name Jesus.

Breaking News: "Our news affiliate in Bethlehem is reporting today the mass murder of young children by Herod, the governor of Galilee and Roman-appointed King of the Jews. Unverified reports indicate that jealousy for his throne by a baby born to an unwed teenage mother named Mary of Nazareth and her husband Joseph have prompted the killings. Foreign Persian astrologers claim to have been following a star to pay homage to the baby who they believe to be a future King of the Jews. Prior to the birth Mary's cousin Elizabeth was sure that Mary's baby was unique. She was pregnant herself with a baby conceived after menopause with her elderly husband, a temple priest.

Reports indicate that Mary's pregnancy was the result of a 'holy spirit.' There are rumors that an angel told the Jewish peasant her son would continue the throne of a distant relative David, who was king of Israel about one thousand years ago. Also, Mary's boyfriend, Joseph, claims to have seen the same angel in a dream confirming that Mary's baby was not by another man, but by the same holy spirit and that he should marry her anyway. Most townspeople who claim to have heard the rumor about this baby have dismissed it as impossible and that both mother and "father" are out of their minds. The couple and child went missing days ago. Jewish synagogue and temple leaders have not returned our calls. We did find a shepherd who claims to have seen the baby after being told by many angels the child's location. We plan to follow this story to verify the claims that this baby may be the savior of not only the Jews but also of all humanity."

Jesus' birth story is scandalously sensational and would have been today a lead story reported by news pundits everywhere. As we follow Mary's interactions with Jesus throughout her life as his mother, we'll see how conflicted and tense Mary's relationship with Jesus really was. At the same time, we'll note her role in nurturing her child as the mother of God, Jesus of Nazareth, who grew in body, soul, and spirit in her home.

Our quest for the historical Mary is set within the context of a uniquely physiological pregnancy of her cousin Elizabeth; for the text begins, "in the sixth month," that is *Elizabeth's* six month carrying John the Baptizer, Israel's last great prophet.

There is no way Mary was waiting for an angel to announce that she would bear a child who would be king David. Only two people were waiting for Jesus–Simeon and Anna. We'll talk about them later. No religious leaders of any synagogue or temple acknowledged Gabriel's claims about Jesus.

Mary's first reaction after being startled by the presence of an angel in her kitchen was outright fear. She may or may not have known about "the angel of the Lord" speaking to her female ancestors about unusual births–Sarah and her slave woman Hagar, the mothers of Isaac and Ishmael. Sarah's son Isaac would have a unique role ushering in a blessing on humanity directly related to Jesus' role as savior. Hagar's baby, Ishmael, would become a patriarch of Islam centuries later. Like Mary, all women in her family tree were surprised when an angel announced that they would have a son.

Mary response to Gabriel's greeting was not religious. She was not at all initially enamored by his lofty message about her son. A religious response would have been, "Wow, Gabriel, that's awesome; you mean I'm going to be the mother of the long-awaited Messiah? I can't wait to tell my mother and my girlfriends. Will the Holy Spirit really overshadow me like the misty glory over the Tabernacle in the desert? This is going to be a spiritual high. I can't wait." As a Mediterranean woman, the one goal of her life was to save herself for marriage. Gabriel's message assaulted her personhood and presented a biological impossibility. She had found mister wonderful in Joseph. They were about to be married in the cultural sense of that word where she'd be provided for by her husband. They surely talked about having a family. But this was not how they planned it.   How would she tell her mother that she got pregnant by a holy spirit? How would this make her father feel about Joseph? Who'd even believe it? Did she believe it? Mary's anxiety and fear overshadowed any pious feelings about being so favored by God.

God was asking her to have an illegitimate child! How could he do this to her? Mary's real issue was biology, not religion. To go along with Gabriel's proposal would challenge her cultural beliefs and violate her body. She couldn't imagine anyone being happy for her pregnancy. Would anyone of the ladies at the synagogue give her a baby shower?

Notice that initially Gabriel gave Mary no choice about this pregnancy. He said, "You *will* be with child." Since God pleased with her, she was told she'd become pregnant. Whatever happened to the conversations she and Joseph may have had about when they'd plan their first child and future family. How would they like to space their children? Wouldn't they want to get financial settled before their first baby? The conversation about bringing God down to earth began with no apparent regard for how Mary felt about it. God appeared to be challenging Mary's desire to remain a virgin. What did overshadowing really mean physically for her body?

Note the inadequacy of angel Gabriel's attempt to calm her down. Mary wasn't buying it. Gabriel knew he couldn't go back to God with a "no" from Mary; so he had to try logic to convince Mary to heed his message. He used an apples to oranges comparison of Elizabeth's unique pregnancy to Mary's. Elizabeth conceived John the Baptizer by having sexual intercourse with her husband. There was no miracle attached to this conception. Zechariah's sperm impregnated one of Elizabeth's eggs and she was in the sixth month of a normal human pregnancy. The only unique aspect of her conception was that she was past menopause. That's all. Every now and then we hear today about this type of pregnancy. Mary's was the only so-called virgin birth in recorded world history. There is no way Elizabeth's conception is a one-to- one comparison with a holy spirit overshadowing Mary. Elizabeth's conception is explained biologically. Mary's pregnancy defies science.

Please note that the supernatural element in Gabriel's message is not that Mary would have a so-called "virgin birth." That would only claim that no male sperm impregnated Mary's egg resulting in a human being in her womb. The angel's message is that, if I may be forgiven, God would get Mary pregnant using the mysterious language of "come upon" or "overshadowed." The point is that God would be the agent of Jesus' birth, not merely the process. A virgin birth was the process, but not evidence that God was involved. Just like an empty tomb is no evidence that God raised Jesus from the dead. A virgin birth doesn't make God necessary any more than an empty tomb makes God the agent of Jesus' resurrection. Mary's understandable concern was about her body. So we validate Mary's justifiable feelings of initial fear, anxiety, and doubt. Because when it comes to God's intervention in our lives we too have our fears, anxieties, and doubts. Mary gives us permission to have the same questions about God that she had. But she doesn't stay there.

Gabriel's words, "For all things are possible with God" is what started Mary thinking less about her body and more about God. She thought to herself, "If all things with God are possible, maybe even this awkward conception is also possible however outlandish it sounds." She doesn't forget about the consequences of obeying God with her body. She continues to think of herself–but differently. Please get what follows in the next sentence because it's so important for a healthy concept of both ourselves and God.

Mary does not deny her body to be spiritual as an obedient Christian. She's not a gnostic. What happens to Mary's physical body is directly related to God having the body he needs to save the world. Both Mary's body and God's body are integral to what we will later call the incarnation. Mary's doubts turned into belief when she saw herself *in relationship to God*. We know this from her, "I am the Lord's servant." No longer is she alone as a young woman confined to her thoughts about herself and her body. Her fear dissipates, her questions are answered and she's ready to obey because she realizes that God is God and she is not. She wasn't about to tell God his idea of saving the world is misguided or that he should find someone else. The awkward consequences, the gossip in the village, the questions from Joseph, the concern of her parents–all these become less important to her than being the Lord's servant.

At this moment in the conversation Mary takes her place in the long line of patriarchs, matriarchs, and prophets paralleling Moses' ultimate obedience after a barrage of doubts and questions or Isaiah's "Here am I, send me." Mary courageously demonstrates unwavering faith in Yahweh, the God of Abraham, Isaac and Jacob, the great "I AM." Even though she doesn't know all the details, Mary obeys. Her initial fears and doubts give way to peace and faith. "Be it unto me as you have said." Luther maintains that this is the moment of Mary's conception. No one really knows. We're told that Gabriel left for heaven to tell God the good news.

The details are about to unfold, even though Mary is on a learning curve to completely believe that the baby she will deliver is the son of God. Most of this book is a record of her conflicts with her son over the very fact that he is both her human son and the son of God. Being God's mother wasn't going to be easy. We can only imagine as well what all this means for Joseph. He will be a "father" without being a father. Throughout his life Jesus will speak of his father without referencing Joseph. Joseph will teach Jesus how to make a chair and Jesus will talk about being about his father's business without mentioning carpentry. Tension will characterize this parent-child relationship right up to the cross.

We need to mention Matthew's perspective of Joseph's involvement as it relates to Mary. He gets a special audience with an angel to explain Mary's pregnancy. We find a caring boyfriend who seeks only his future's wife's safety. One aspect of Jewish law would have had her stoned to death. If Joseph considered divorcing her, something God hates, he abandons Mary in shame. When he takes her home, Mary becomes his wife avoiding both shame and death.

Finally, the Matthew text states "but before they came together" and "he had no union with her until after she gave birth to a son." Both statements strongly imply that Joseph and Mary began fulfilling the biblical definition of marriage about "becoming one flesh." There is no reason to deny Mary's humanity to enjoy having children after having Jesus. As a Jewish woman, Mary would consider having other children as God's blessing on her life. We'll get into specific references to Mary's other children later in the book. By having children after Jesus, she obeyed the creation mandate to replenish the earth with human beings created in the image of God. Jesus' younger siblings ultimately became members of the church along with their mother all of whom recognized him as their Savior. It is the human Mary of the Gospels who is favored by God, not a ceramic Mary created in the image of religious legend.

To conclude we've launched a discussion about the greatest birth story amidst scandal and faith complete with fear, anxiety, and doubt turned into peace, trust, and belief. We've presented the real Mary of history–an ordinary human being called to an extraordinary mission by God. Of course, the protagonist in the drama of world salvation is Jesus of Nazareth, Mary's son. But God chose her to make God visible on earth with a body. She chose to participate in God's plan once she understood who she was in relationship to God; namely, his servant. Then she quickly obeyed. Mary encourages our faith. We can easily relate to her initial fears and doubts. Who among us has not had similar feelings when sorting out what God is doing in our lives? We've positioned Mary as an ordinary sinner requiring the same grace that any of us needs. It is by God's grace, not because of her purity, that Gabriel announces her role. She will continue to have questions throughout the drama told in the following pages. At this point, Mary still requires assurance. We turn now to the next part of the story where during a visit with an understanding cousin, Mary receives her first blessing as the mother of God.

Chapter 2

Blessed

Luke 1: 39–45, 56

Right after Gabriel visited Mary, she hurried off into the hill country to see her cousin Elizabeth. Elizabeth heard Mary's greeting and was filled with the Holy Spirit. Her baby actually leaped in her womb. In a loud voice she exclaimed, "Blessed are you among women, and blessed is the child you will bear! Why am I so favored that the mother of my Lord should come to me? Just as the sound of your greeting reached my ears, my baby leaped for joy. Blessed is she who has believed that the Lord will do what he has said!"

Mary stayed with Elizabeth for about three months and then returned home.

Gabriel left as quickly as he appeared. Mary was still in shock. "What have I just agreed to?" She had to be feeling so alone with hundreds of questions racing through her mind. Who should she tell first? Her mother, Joseph, her father or her girlfriends? She couldn't just keep it all inside. Then she remembered that Gabriel mentioned cousin Elizabeth. Though she wasn't as convinced as the angel that Elizabeth's pregnancy was exactly like hers, maybe Elizabeth would understand what she was going through. Elizabeth would be the first person Mary told about the angelic message. Maybe Elizabeth as an unlettered country-woman bearing Israel's last prophet would understand how she felt as the soon-to-be mother, a peasant engaged to a carpenter. The synagogue leaders would have only laughed her to scorn. Nothing in Judaism predicted the roles of Elizabeth and Mary in the drama associated with ushering in Israel's liberator. Mary would feel more confident about Gabriel's message only after she had talked with Elizabeth.

Elizabeth had six more months than Mary to grasp her late-in-life pregnancy. While Scripture records only her brief greeting to Mary, they had three months to talk about their experience. Mary stayed with Elizabeth right through the delivery of her son John. She'd now be able to return to face her future husband, family, and friends buttressed by Elizabeth's wisdom and encouragement. Did she realize John's role as the greatest promoter of Jesus' ministry?

Elizabeth also knew that God favored her. For too long she'd been unable to have a child. But after her husband's "come to God" moment in the temple with Gabriel, she and Zechariah became pregnant. Elizabeth's joy revolved around having a child. She was delighted to become pregnant, unlike Mary's initial response of fear and anxiety. After all, Elizabeth would have her child like Sarah and Hannah as a married woman who God had now chosen to bless after years of trying. Mary's pregnancy would be scandalous; she'd feel far less "favored." This is why Gabriel's attempt to compare Mary's too-early-in-life pregnancy with Elizabeth's was limited and made sense only as an example that God could do the impossible. Have any two mothers ever had exactly the same experience of conception, labor, and delivery?

Gabriel's visits to both Mary and Zechariah had similarities as well as differences. Let's get into the backstory of Zechariah the priest's experience with Gabriel. He, like Mary, was in fear when an angel just showed up at the altar. Note the parallels in these two angelic visits. Both sang about the birth of their sons. However, note also the differences. Gabriel comes only to the husband with the good news that his barren wife would have a child. Gabriel comes to both Joseph and Mary with the news about Jesus. Elizabeth gets her information second-hand without direct contact with an angel. There's really no need to over-analyze this difference except to say that Joseph received from Gabriel the assurance he needed to keep from being suspicious about Mary's pregnancy. Gabriel offered Joseph comfort but challenged Zechariah's disbelief which had consequences–an inability to speak. Note that Mary's question "How can this be?" had no visible consequences, probably because in a matter of seconds she changed her mind. Of course, Elizabeth would have *wanted* to hear news about having a child. Mary was totally unprepared for such news. Elizabeth's would be a sign of blessing to all. Mary's would only raise embarrassing questions requiring lots of difficult answers.

Elizabeth was the courageous woman Mary needed. While Luke details John the Baptizer's birth story from his father's perspective, the little mention he gives Elizabeth is nevertheless significant. Elizabeth stands up to both family and friends at the naming ceremony of her son. Her tongue-tied husband was of no help as the politics of naming her baby swirled around the kitchen table. She knew her baby's name needed to be John. But how? Zechariah came home dumb after spending a week in the temple doing his priestly duty. He couldn't talk about what had happened in the temple. Maybe he had to write it out. Luke doesn't tell us. We do know that Zechariah later wrote out that the baby would be called John. Elizabeth was all alone against lots of people who wanted to follow tradition naming the baby after a relative. Elizabeth was both a woman of courage and faith. There's a good chance that Mary observed all this as a member of the family. It was a confidence-builder for her at just the right time. Now let's get into the documented conversation we have between two of the most important Jewish women in history; one, the mother of Israel's last prophet, the other, the mother of God.

Here we have Mary doing the greeting with incredible results. We don't know what Mary said but it had two remarkable consequences; first, Elizabeth is said to have to have been filled with the Holy Spirit and second, her baby leaped in her womb. Unlike Mary's and Zechariah's responses of fear at an angel's greeting, Elizabeth shouts for joy and her baby does acrobatics in her womb. So what does it mean to be "filled with the Holy Spirit?" We need to trace this supernatural phenomenon going back into Jewish history.

The first mention of being filled with a holy spirit, who is named as the Holy Spirit, the third person of the triune God, occurs in the Torah to a craftsman for the furniture to be placed in the tabernacle, a tent the mobile nation used for worship as it traveled from Egypt to the promise land. Most of the language in the Old Testament speaks of this spiritual experience occurring over the tabernacle or in the temple itself. Do you remember the word *overshadow* in reference to Mary's conception? This is exactly the same spiritual phenomenon going back to the early days of Israel's escape from Egypt. The use of "overshadowed" isn't accidental. The presence of God came over Mary in the same way the Holy Spirit overshadowed the tent of meeting. Just as an obscure tabernacle craftsman was filled with God's presence, Elizabeth was overcome with the Spirit's filling when Mary greeted her. Mary's visit occasions a profoundly spiritual experience for Elizabeth as her older cousin mentors and encourages this young confused mother-to-be.

Mary's observation of Elizabeth's experience of the Holy Spirit had to be both startling and encouraging. Startling because this would be the first time she's been near someone having this experience. Encouraging because this is precisely how she would conceive her baby. It was a joyous event! She could begin to rest assured that such an encounter with Jehovah need not be threatening. Whether Mary was pregnant or not during this visit, we do not know. The point is that Mary was gaining confidence and affirmation from Elizabeth confirming Gabriel's message. Mary's awareness of her baby's identity evolved throughout her life. That her son was both human and God created conflict and tension. Elizabeth was the first person in a long line of encouragers and supporters who confirmed Mary's role in bringing the savior to earth. Nothing in the biblical witness leads us to believe that Mary had some overnight "a-hah" moment and had this all figured out. The human Mary of the Bible, the only one who ever existed, didn't approach these early days from any religious tradition. Nothing in her religious tradition confirmed her experience. In fact, everything about her experience opposed Jewish understanding of who the messiah would be, how he would arrive and what he would do once he showed up. It would take Mary quite a while to grasp all this. Just like you and I have needed lots of time to understand how God intervenes and works in *our* lives. This is why Mary is so good for us. Not a piously religious Mary who has it altogether. But the human Mary of Nazareth whose courageously obedient life challenged her religious tradition.

Elizabeth blesses Mary. She's the first to do so and fulfils what Mary would later sing about during her visit. "Bless" can become a dangerous word if used inappropriately. It can imply worship, adoration, and praise. Or, it can simply mean to request God's power upon someone. "Bless" as worship can only refer to God; "bless" as empowerment is appropriate for another human being. Elizabeth blesses Mary by affirming God's power upon her as the mother of God compared to all other women. Any interpretation of this event in Mary's life which suggests that Elizabeth worshiped Mary misunderstands what's really happening. Historic religious tradition hasn't always gotten Mary right. Nothing in Scripture urges the church to worship Mary. She never claims worship for herself. We'll see this more clearly in the next chapter as she's caught up in enthusiastic worship and praise to God. When Elizabeth blesses the fruit of Mary's womb knowing that the child is her Lord, she may very well be worshiping a baby *in utero*; for that baby is God.

Elizabeth's next statement is a theological breakthrough. Her use of "my Lord" is new language in Judaism for it personalizes one's expression of relationship with God unprecedented in Israel's history. Only as Jesus arrives on the scene does one with faith in the God of Abraham, Isaac, and Jacob have a personal intimate relationship with the Ineffable One, the great I AM. The name of Elizabeth's God is unspeakable until Mary has her baby. Just as

Elizabeth's baby is the forerunner of Messiah, she here anticipates how the church will refer to Jesus in a personal way, as "Abba, Father." Mary can't do this for Elizabeth, but her baby will. This is why the church can say, "Our Father" when reciting the Lord's Prayer.

Finally, Elizabeth's blessing has a specific basis. She affirms the reason for blessing her cousin Mary because of her belief in God's word. Elizabeth affirms Mary's trust in the Lord that he will not only conceive her baby but also see to it that she delivers her baby. Elizabeth encourages Mary in her faith to go along with the message from the angel that her son will continue the throne of their famous relative David. Mary has no idea at this time what it might mean that David's throne will be eternal. She demonstrates faith when she can't grasp all the details or meanings about the jarring events in her recent life. She knows she's God's servant. She's ready to obey. She's been affirmed by a wiser cousin just at the right time in this confusing transition. In so doing, Mary continues to model what it means to be a disciple of Jesus the Messiah. In fact, she's so excited about her visit with Elizabeth that she breaks out into exuberant praise and song to which we now turn our attention.

Chapter 3

Ecstatic

Luke 1: 46–55

During her visit with Elizabeth, Mary sang, "My soul glorifies the Lord and my spirit rejoices in God my Savior, for he has been mindful of his servant's humble state. From now on all generations will call me blessed, for the Mighty One has done great things for me–holy is his name. His mercy extends to those who fear him, from generation to generation. He has performed mighty deeds with his arm; he has scattered those who are proud in their inmost thoughts. He has brought down rulers from their thrones but has lifted up the humble. He has filled the hungry with good things but has sent the rich away empty. He has helped his servant Israel, remembering to be merciful to Abraham and his descendants forever, even as he said to our fathers."

THE HUMAN MARY IS not a static porcelain figurine in a nativity scene. She's ecstatic [literally "beside herself"] in joyful song at the end of her visit with Elizabeth. She's a dynamic personality experiencing changes in mood, emotion and feeling as she becomes more aware that her child is the son of God. We've seen her go from fear and disbelief to trust and obedience. It was a vulnerable young mother-to-be who required mentoring from an older wiser member of her family going through her own "surprise" pregnancy. While Mary visited Elizabeth, a huge breakthrough occurs in her relationship with God. In fact, it is so profound that she must sing it because the spoken word fails to express her joy. Traditionally, the church has called her song the *Magnificat* where she sings of God's greatness, holiness, and mercy.

There's a Jewish tradition for emotional prayer, singing, and dancing when God has done great things for an individual or for the nation. When 90-year-old Sarah delivered her son Isaac, she just laughed in wonder. Like Mary she pondered God's grace toward her. The Torah tells us that after crossing the Red Sea on dry ground, Moses sang a long hymn exalting the Lord as his salvation. Miriam, a prophetess, repeated the hymn and led a line dance of women singing with tambourines. When Hannah discovered she was pregnant, she prayed a praise song which anticipates the very stanzas Mary would use a millennium later. Elizabeth's husband, Zechariah sang praises to God after getting his speech back at the naming ceremony of his son, John.

Mary cannot be reduced to a timid Mediterranean young women protecting her virginity, tending the hearth and working a loom as a dutiful homemaker. When Luther read her song, he called her the virgin-scholar. She boldly sings the Word of God recounting God's acts in the history of Israel. She's "beside herself" in joy. She's filled with the Holy Spirit taking a page from Elizabeth's greeting and extending it into a hymn. Gone is Mary's fearful doubting.. She's not questioning an angel, but singing like one. God has used Elizabeth to move Mary along in her deepening relationship with Yahweh. Mary is getting ready to deliver the son of God, her savior.

She uses uncommon vocabulary. Normal Jewish worshippers never sang or spoke so personally about their relationship with God. Recall that traditionally, God was the unspoken Ineffable One. Yahweh was represented without vowels in their writings to ensure that no one would try to say his name. How would you say YHWH? As exuberant as Miriam's and Hannah's songs were, they do not mention God as "my savior." Zechariah's hymn of thanksgiving is really a Jewish benediction and contains nothing intimate about his personal relationship with God. Mary is breaking tradition and runs the risk of disrespecting the Lord. Mary is the first human being to claim that God is her Savior. If you've ever sung about God as your Savior, you can thank Mary. She started it. Let's take a brief look at how Mary sings about who God is and what he's done in her life. That's right, the young peasant woman from Nazareth is a theologian.

Mary uses the first person five times in her song's first stanza–"my soul, my spirit, my Savior, call me blessed, and for me." This is abnormal Jewish hymnody. Jewish songs were far less autobiographical. Typically, a Jewish hymn would begin with profound words of adoration and praise about God's attributes. Mary will go there as well, but not until she intimately expresses herself personally. Remember that Mary's baby is Jesus. It will be Mary's son who teaches his disciples how to pray, saying "*Our* Father. . .," not merely *the* Father. The Apostle Paul will later remind the church that we have every right to call Yahweh, "Daddy." Mary is the first disciple to teach us how to address God personally. Elizabeth referred to God as her Lord; Mary is the first human being to address God as her savior. Christians have been doing so ever since.

Mary's use of "blessed" deserves some attention. She says that all future generations will call her blessed. Let's first discuss what Mary is not saying. This is not her way of saying future Christians will worship her. God dignifies Mary as his mother; he doesn't deify her! The term Mary uses implies one's desire to see that another person enjoys the benefits of God in her life. So, as a member of one of those future generations, when I bless Mary I'm recalling the grace that God extended to her. Her desire for future generations would be that we never forget how good God was to her. Note that she caps off this first stanza with one of the most profoundly exalted attributes for God–he is holy. I think she said that just in case one of those future generations would confuse *worshiping* with *blessing*. The only claim Mary ever made about herself is that future Christians should bless her, not idolize her with statues or circle her head with haloes.

The second stanza of the *Magnificat* speaks of God's historical acts. She begins by praising God for his mercy. Possibly she recalls the Torah's reminder that God has mercy upon whoever he wants. Mary thanks God for being merciful to her and to all who revere the Lord. Maybe she has David in mind in his classic psalm of confession where he credits God for his mercy and forgiveness. Mary had to have known her "Bible" to list these powerful statements about God. Her reference to God's arm doing mighty deeds is stated every year in the Seder Passover feast where Israel's escape from Egyptian captivity is accomplished by God's strong right hand. So Mary knew that the central event in Judaism was release from Egyptian slavery. Her hymn of praise anticipated Wesley's words, "my chains fell off, my heart was free." Would she have realized that her baby boy would liberate all humanity through his death and resurrection? When she sang about God scattering those who are proud, did she realize how self-righteous religious leaders of the temple who would speak against her son? Recall that the teachers of the law were always scheming how to trap Jesus. Mary had to be aware of how God toppled Assyrian and Babylonian kings who took Israel captive. She uses a loving and compassionate tone which anticipates her baby's future ministry. Jesus launched his ministry by quoting Isaiah. It sounds like the *Magnificat*.

In Luke 4: 18–19, we are told that Jesus read the following in a synagogue:

> The Spirit of the Lord is on me, because he has anointed me to preach good news to the poor. He has sent me to proclaim freedom for prisoners and recovery of sight for the blind; to release the oppressed and to proclaim the year of the Lord's favor.

Note how the above words parallel Mary's compassionate tone. The content and spirit of both Mary's song and Jesus' manifesto for ministry align perfectly. It would be interesting to know whether mother Mary would have discussed her song after hearing Jesus read these words. I believe a case may be made for how Mary influenced Jesus' ministry. Did Jesus grow in wisdom, knowledge, and grace while nurtured by his mother? Of course. As we follow Jesus' ministry we know of his preference for the poor, marginalized, and destitute. Mary's sense of justice and compassion permeates this song. When Jesus' disciples ministered to the marginalized, they unknowingly ministered to him.

Matthew records that Jesus talked with his followers about sheep and goats. The sheep were those who loved anyone by feeding him, giving him water when he was thirsty, offering him hospitality as a stranger, clothing him, caring for him when he was ill and visiting him when went to prison. But Jesus fed thousands, claimed to be living water, stayed with relatives and friends, never got sick, and never went to prison. Who was he talking about? His followers had no recollection that they ever did that for him. Jesus replied that when they did all these things for the poor and marginalized, they did it for him. So in our society today, we may think of the homeless beggar on a street corner as Jesus himself. This final judgement story challenged his followers to abandon their self-righteous religion and to love others as they loved Christ. Jesus began his ministry with words from Luke and concluded his teaching about the kingdom with Matthew. Each text is anticipated in Mary's exuberant song of praise to God.

Mary's *Magnificat* is important for at least two reasons. First, it's a huge turning point in her relationship with God. From Gabriel's greeting to this song, she has gone from fear to ecstasy. Second, it suggests one way Mary may have influenced Jesus' ministry. Could she have discussed this with her son during his development or sung it to him as a lullaby? Of course, she'd have to tone it down a bit if she wanted him to go to sleep! Think about the impact of Jesus hearing this song every night during the formative years of his life. As with many mothers, Mary's prayers and songs influenced her child's life and ministry. Just as Mary's awareness of her son's identity s God evolved, Jesus' wisdom and grace grew as the unique God-human. So far we've had our discussions of Jesus in Mary's womb. It's now time for Mary to have her baby. She'll get morning sick, get back pains, endure labor and finally deliver a baby with an umbilical cord who will turn from blue to red as oxygen permeates his crying body–the body that Mary gave him so he could be God on earth. It is to this highest point in her life that we now turn our attention.

Chapter 4

Contemplative

Luke 2: 1–20

When Caesar Augustus decreed a census, people had to return to their own town. Joseph and Mary went from Nazareth to Bethlehem, the town of David, to register. They were engaged and Mary was expecting a child. While in Bethlehem, Mary delivered her firstborn son in the stable of a guesthouse because there was no other place to sleep. She wrapped him in cloths and used a limestone manger for his crib. As usual, shepherds tended their flocks all night outside Bethlehem, when all of a sudden an angel of the Lord appeared to them and the glory of God shone all around them. The shepherds were terrified! But the angel told them not to be afraid and said, "I bring you the Gospel, good news of great joy, for all people. Today a baby boy, a Savior, is born in Bethlehem, the town of David. He is Christ, the Messiah. He will be the baby wrapped in cloths lying in a manger." Then a great company of the heavenly host of angels appeared praising God, saying, "Glory to God in the highest and peace on earth to all people of goodwill!" After the angels went back to heaven, the shepherds said, "Let's go to Bethlehem to see if what we've been told has actually happened." So they hurried off and found Mary,

Joseph and the baby wrapped in cloths lying in a manger. Having seen him, they spread the word about Jesus. Everybody got really excited–except Mary. She quietly treasured and pondered all these things in her heart. The shepherds glorified and praised God because all that they had seen and heard from the angels about Jesus was true.

The birth of Jesus is the zenith of Mary's young life. She quietly treasured and pondered all these things in her heart. She remembered everything. We can be sure that what Luke records is accurate because he had access to Mary's baby book as a source for his gospel. The earliest date we have for Luke's writing is around fifty AD. Since both he and Mary, then about sixty-five, were contemporaries, it's likely that he could have interviewed Mary about all those things she continually kept in her heart. As a historian and doctor Luke was a detail person. Mary knew every detail of her pre-birth experience just like every mother. Mothers never forget the birth stories of their babies. Luke's accurate and detailed account of Jesus' birth is a direct result of Mary's memory. Note that the first three vignettes that you've just read span only nine months. As we've seen, a lot happened to Mary during this short period of time but we can be sure she didn't forget a thing. In this chapter we'll get into both the conversations Mary had and the events in her busy life before having her baby. We'll attempt to "connect the dots" as she might have since *pondering* implies meditation upon what she heard during conversations she had with an angel and Elizabeth. Note that Mary told only Elizabeth about Gabriel's message, although we may infer that she told everything to Joseph, but only after returning from her visit to Elizabeth.

What words and conversations might Mary have treasured and pondered in her heart? Let's remember that there were few if any quiet moments in her life until after she delivered Jesus. A jarring visit in her kitchen by Gabriel followed by a hurried visit involving a long journey to Elizabeth's home. Composing the *Magnificat* which may have involved some Torah study, possibly observing John's birth before she left for home, and the long trip to

Bethlehem followed by a search for a room. The only time she may have had to meditate may have been during her travels.

We begin by going back to her conversation with the angel Gabriel. It couldn't have taken more than one minute. During that brief time, Mary reacted with little time to weigh Gabriel's words. Her questions were immediate and couched in the obvious physiological impossibility of a pregnancy without sexual intercourse. Now that she had delivered her baby conceived, she may have asked herself, "What was I so afraid of" or "Why wasn't I happier with being chosen to usher in the messiah–every Jewish girl's dream?"

Then she discovered that Elizabeth's husband, Zechariah the priest, had a similar conversation with Gabriel. When Mary discovered the words to his hymn of praise about his wife's unique but not miraculous pregnancy, she may have connected the dots on the relationship between her son and her cousin's baby. Would it be a stretch for her to marvel at God's mighty acts going on at the same time within her family? Mary needed to confirm what the angel told her about Elizabeth having a late-in-life baby. When Elizabeth greeted her as she did, a greeting of joy not fear, Mary started putting things together. Maybe she really *was* going to have a son who was God.

Her mood and emotion shifted from quiet acceptance of God's will to ecstatic praise in song. Mary never sang like this before! Something to ponder. Was she aware of Isaiah's prophecy that his wife, a young woman, would have a son who foreshadowed her as a virgin having Jesus, as Matthew records? More specifically, did she remember that in only a few words later the prophet speaks of a son who will reign on David's throne eternally just like Gabriel said? Wow! Was her baby boy really the savior of the world, the messiah? Let's not forget that Mary was the first to name Jesus as God her savior. That's why Luke later wrote that Mary's baby would come to seek out and to save all humanity. As she dictated all these words to Luke, a gentile, did she remember what God said to father Abraham about all nations being blessed through his family? Another wow! This time of contemplation and recollection began to formulate in Mary's mind all those great things God had done for her–recall the first stanza of her praise song.

"Why was I so worried about Joseph's reaction to my being with child?" If nothing was impossible with God, wouldn't he provide Joseph the same peace of mind? Whatever doubt Mary may have had, and it was only human that she did, she now had the time to quietly reflect that God knew what he was doing. She was beginning to truly believe. This is why the human Mary of the Scriptures is so helpful to us. We, too, need time to mull and reflect on God's words to us during difficult events in our lives. We need to take a page out of Mary's baby book.

Mary might have thought, "Wasn't Joseph's courageous to take me home sparing my life?" Note how Joseph, the most underrated actor in the drama of world redemption is no longer mentioned so early in Jesus' life. We don't know what happened to him. Some suggest he died soon after. One of the things Mary may have treasured in her heart was her husband's love for her. She felt protected and provided for–like any wife wants to feel.

Jesus did not virtually come out of Mary's body in some mystical way. She carried Jesus for nine months, needed regular backrubs and her water broke beginning her labor pains. Any religious attempt to portray Mary as impervious to the pain of childbirth has no basis in the biblical witness. Baby Jesus arrived on earth through Mary's birth canal. The beauty of Jesus' birth is all about the ordinariness of his mother, not some virtual magic involved in her baby's delivery. She experienced everything any woman would when giving birth. Mary was processing a lot while she recovered her strength and composure right after her delivery. That transition pain and the delivery, with or without a midwife, had its moments of agony. But she was smiling now. The hard part was over as Jesus lay on her breasts right after birth prior to resting him in that crude feeding trough for an ox. Mary strained and pushed to deliver the savior to the world. Mary counted Jesus' fingers and toes; they were all there. It was a boy! She was exhausted and relieved. Mary felt a deep sense of fulfillment. She had lots to ponder.

Smelly shepherds were the first evangelists of the Gospel. How might their grasp of raising sacrificial sheep made more sense to them when an angel told them about a savior? Would they live long enough to hear Israel's last prophet, John, point out that the baby they found was the last lamb who would need to be sacrificed for sin and sinners? It was too early for even Mary to make this connection. Now was a time for joy at the savior's birth. Mary was consistently put into the position of having to assess the truth of every statement she heard either from an angel, Elizabeth or now at Jesus' birth from shepherds.

Shepherds played an unusual role in Mary's life. They conveyed a divine message to her at Jesus' rough-hewn cradle. Possibly just after she had nursed her baby for the first time and put him down for a nap, she may have had to quiet that herd of shepherds at her door. They had just searched for a baby in a manger. Of all things, it would be a manger that identified the infant son of God. Mary's first response to cribbing Jesus in a manger was most likely negative. How unclean! No mother today would do so. An unsanitary cradle identified the messiah. She had to have pondered this and resolved once again that God knew what he was doing. Mary may have even had to get over all the noise of excited shepherds. "Don't wake up the baby!" Then maybe later while contemplating Jesus' birth, she may have been heartened by the role excited shepherds played in getting the message about her son.

Luke agrees with Matthew that Jesus was Mary's firstborn. What does this mean? In the Bible *firstborn* may be used either humanly or divinely according to context. The Apostle Paul use the term referring to the privileges Jesus Christ enjoys as the firstborn of all creation. He extends the meaning from human to divine just as the first son born to a Jewish mother had privileges no subsequent son had. He uses the term divinely within a context of extolling the supremacy of Christ over everything. But here the context is about a human birth to mother Mary having her first child. Would he have even mentioned *firstborn* if Jesus were Mary's only child? No.

No historical research supports that Jesus was an only child. There is no reason to doubt that Mary of Nazareth enjoyed a healthy sexual relationship with Joseph throughout their marriage. Recall that Matthew states that Joseph had no union with Mary *until she gave birth to a son*. Why would he say this if Mary remained a virgin throughout her marriage? Any tradition of the church which seeks to perpetuate Mary's virginity unnecessarily denies her humanity. If perpetuating Mary's virginity is thought to keep her pure, then sexual intercourse itself must be impure. That's absurd. Sexual intercourse is God's design for populating the earth with people to care for animals and plants. God's methods are not impure. Mary's devotion to God included her desire for her husband and her faithfulness only to him. Her sexual relationship with her husband resulting in Jesus' siblings had no impact upon her purity as the mother of God.

Mary was well aware of the definition of marriage from the Torah which talked about a woman and a man cleaving to one another and becoming one flesh. The only mention of Mary's purity in Scripture involves her Jewish culture's ritual of cleansing after childbirth. That ritual dictated the time for an important Jewish ceremony–the dedication of a firstborn son in the temple. We now to turn to that memorable event which would prove to be bitter-sweet.

Chapter 5

Wondered

Luke 2: 21-40

Mary named her baby Jesus as Gabriel had said and had him circumcised when he was eight days old. When Mary completed her purification according to the Law of Moses, they took him to the temple in Jerusalem to present him to the Lord. The Torah stated that every firstborn male is to be consecrated offering a sacrifice of either two doves or two young pigeons.

Simeon, a righteous and devout man was in the temple waiting for the consolation of Israel. The Holy Spirit was upon him and revealed to Simeon that he would see the Messiah before he died.

Led by the Spirit, he went into the temple courts, and met Joseph and Mary. He took Jesus into his arms and praised God saying, "Sovereign Lord, as you have promised, now dismiss your servant in peace. For I have seen the salvation you've prepared in the sight of all people as a light for revelation to the Gentiles and for the glory of your people Israel."

Mary and Joseph marveled at his words. Simeon then blessed them and said to Mary, "This child will be spoken against because he will reveal the thoughts of many hearts. As a sign he is destined to cause the falling and rising of many in Israel. A sword will pierce your heart also."

An eighty four year old prophetess, Anna, was also in the temple. She was a widow after only seven years of marriage. She worshiped, fasted and prayed night and day, never leaving the temple. Just as Simeon had completed his blessing, Anna came over to them giving thanks to God and spoke about the child to all who were looking forward to the redemption of Jerusalem.

After doing everything required by the Law of the Lord, Joseph and Mary returned to Nazareth.

Jesus grew and became strong, was filled with wisdom, and God's grace was upon him.

JESUS' DEDICATION IN THE temple was a turning point in Mary's life. So far her fast-paced existence over the last nine months had improved with each event we've discussed. Gabriel's message changed her life in ways she never thought possible. But she believed that all things are possible with God and submitted to his will. Though a bit bewildered, she had a mentor in cousin Elizabeth who blessed and affirmed her as the mother of God. Elizabeth may have believed this more than Mary at the time. During this visit we hear Mary singing at the top of her lungs in ecstatic worship to God her savior. Mary's life got only better going from the annunciation to the *Magnificat*. The high point in Mary's life was giving birth to Jesus of Nazareth, the son of God. Everything came together offering her a meaningful time of meditation and contemplation.

Eight days after Jesus' birth she named her baby and had him circumcised according to Jewish law and ritual. Forty days after Jesus' birth Joseph and Mary brought their son to the temple to give him back to God. The Torah required that every firstborn son be given back to God in a religious ceremony at the temple. This ceremony originated as an act of gratitude, since every Jewish firstborn was "passed-over" by the angel of death when every Egyptian firstborn was killed.

Every new Jewish mother also knew that she needed to bathe over a period of thirty days before she could entered the temple. Just like her first reaction to Gabriel's message was one of shock and humility because God would favor her a sinner, Mary participated in the purification ritual like any ordinary practicing Jewess at the time. She humbly and obediently purified herself according to Jewish law. Both Joseph and Mary followed the law's requirement to bring a sacrifice. If you were rich, you brought a lamb; if you were poor, two pigeons or two turtledoves. Mary and Joseph were poor.

Mary's life radically changed after presenting Jesus to God. From this point on we'll observe a downward spiral during misunderstanding with her son accompanied by feelings of frustration. It's appropriate that we do. Primarily because Scripture records a human Mary unsullied by the church. Second, because Mary is human like us, we can all relate to her as a credible follower of Jesus. Her quiet pondering after his birth would now be interrupted by raising a child who happened to be messiah. How would you like to raise the savior of the world? Intimidated? Threatened? Nervous? Afraid that if you do something wrong, you might negatively impact saving all humanity? These feelings may have been Mary's as she received new information about her life and her son's.

The text mentions two people who play a significant role in Mary's life during the dedication, even though neither is an official of the temple. Simeon was a devout man and Anna a prophetess. They were the only people on earth who were looking for messiah. Parenthetically, Mary was caught by surprise by Gabriel's message. Elizabeth needed her own unique pregnancy to begin thinking about a savior, her Lord. Zechariah doubted, Joseph was confused, Herod needed pagan astrologers and there's no record of even one synagogue or temple religious official who acknowledged that Jesus was the predicted messiah.

Simeon praised God for allowing him to see Jesus. It was on his bucket list. It was all he wanted before he died. He started out with a heartfelt statement of praise to God noting that this baby would fulfil God's promise to bless all humanity, Gentiles and Jews. The couple was positively encouraged with his words. But Mary had to wonder about the mixed message which followed. While calling down God's gracious power upon both Joseph and Mary, Simeon turned only to Mary and said that Jesus would trip people up in their religion. The Apostle John would later affirm this prophecy by stating that the very people Jesus came to save would reject him. We can imagine Mary standing there not really sure she wants to give her son back to God if this is what it would mean. Her pondering had to be different from the positive contemplation prior to giving birth. Here her wonder went to possible negative implications about her son.

But there's more. Simeon continued to say that when her son begins teaching, even the teachers of the law will challenge and contradict him. That is, the very leaders of the temple, would become Jesus' enemies. Mary may have wondered why they decided to make the trip to Jerusalem if this is what she was to learn about her son. Not only that, Jesus would expose the religious hypocrisy of those very same people who reject him. Jesus would isolate himself as more authoritative with a gift of discernment into people's hearts and minds. Jesus would be a mind-reader and tell people what we're thinking. In so doing, Jesus would make people look bad; and he'd pay a price for it.

Finally, the last part of Simeon's prophetic word is the most devastating for Mary. Simeon talked about a sword. Where did *that* come from? The price Mary's son would pay for being an incognito messiah will be death. Throughout his life, Jesus would experience insults and demeaning comments. Mary, he implies, would be so hurt by all of this that it will feel like she is being stabbed in the heart.

So much for Jesus' dedication service. Of course, this wasn't a liturgical event. To be fair, Simeon's message wasn't all bad. He did affirm that Jesus would also cause many to rise as well. Looking back through the lens of his life, we see how many people Jesus healed, taught, and encouraged in their faith. The most outstanding positive statement in Simeon's message anticipates Jesus' love for all people on earth–Jews and Gentiles, people of the promise and those outside of the promise. Jesus, he said, would take the scales off the eyes of Gentiles while continuing to glorify the nation of Israel, his own people.

Here Simeon goes back to the Torah and ahead to the Apostles Peter and Paul where Jesus is central. Recall that it is Abraham through whom all families on earth would be blessed. Note that it is Jesus' mother who sings this in the last stanza of the *Magnificat*. We can picture Mary smile knowingly even though we're sure she doesn't have it all figured out. We can't be sure that Mary would have been able to completely get past a political interpretation of Simeon's words. After all, the dominant theme among Jews at the time was hoping for a liberator to deliver them from Roman occupation and the puppet Herods.

In sum, Simeon stated that Jesus would enlighten all humanity and remind Israel that they were God's chosen people. The difficult news for Mary to hear was that her son would be a reason many would struggle in their Jewish faith. That people would speak out publicly against him and reject his teaching. That he would suffer criticism for exposing religious hypocrisy and that he may be killed because of his ministry. It's important to note that Luke uses a word for Simeon's blessing which is best understood as calling down God's gracious power upon the couple. Mary and Joseph would need grace in ways about which they had no idea.

Mary and Joseph really wondered about Simeon's words. In effect Mary's response may have been similar to how she initially reacted to Gabriel's greeting. Back then she was as perplexed and confused as she found herself now. We know that her doubts were resolved by seeing herself as God's servant. But now there was no resolution; only more bewilderment. What could these words really mean about her son? About her? Mary didn't want to believe the negative portion of Simeon's predictions about her child. What mother would? And why would all this have to come out during a dedication service? Didn't she have the right to be happy for her child on the day a mother celebrates giving her son back to God?

Anna lived in the temple worshiping day and night while waiting for the liberation of her city. Anna's comments were shorter and less specific than Simeon's prophecy. Luke never tells us what she said; but it sounded like praying for her city's release from Roman occupation. She, like Simeon, sought the legal and political freedom her people. They both knew this from their study of Israel's prophets. Mary left church that day with a lot to think about. It was a lot more than she bargained for and left too many unanswered questions.

Mary and Joseph had time to think about what they had just learned about their son on their journey back to Bethlehem where they settled into their new home. Having performed all the necessary rituals, they handed down to Jesus the traditions of their faith in preparation for their boy to become a son of the commandments. Luke tells us that Jesus grew physically, intellectually, and spiritually through the influence of his godly parents. We can be sure that this included the nurture of a loving mother and father. Just when Mary might have thought that all the surprises in her life were over and she could settle down to being a mother, they now wondered about a knock on the door from gift-bearing foreigners looking for her son. Would Simeon's prophetic words be fulfilled so soon?

Chapter Six

Conflicted

Matthew 2: 1–12

Months after Jesus was born in Bethlehem in Judea when Herod was king, Magi from the east came to Jerusalem asking, "Where is the one who has been born king of the Jews? We saw his star in the east and have come to worship him." This disturbed King Herod and everyone in Jerusalem. So Herod called together all the chief priests and teachers of the law and asked them where Christ was to be born. They replied, "In Bethlehem in Judea for this is what Micah wrote, 'But you, Bethlehem in the land of Judah are not least among the rulers of Judah; for a ruler who will shepherd my people Israel will from you.' " Herod secretly found out from the Magi exactly when the star appeared and sent them to find the child and report back to him so he could also worship Jesus. The Magi heard the king and traveled to where the star appeared to stop over the house where Jesus was. They saw the child with his mother Mary and bowed down to worship him. Then they opened their gifts of gold, incense and myrrh. Then they went home using a different route having been warned in a dream not to return to Herod.

MARY'S BABY WAS NOW a toddler. The family was living either in a vacated section of the guest-house where Mary delivered Jesus or in their own separate dwelling. We simply don't know. We also can't assume that there were only three Eastern visitors just because we're told that Jesus was given three gifts. Luke calls them Magi which means they might have been Persian or Babylonian astrologers-magicians who continually watched the stars. Mary may have questioned them as to how they even knew about her son being the messiah. After all, she was only gradually beginning to believe it herself. Being aware of rabbinic writings Mary might have been aware that within Judaism the arrival of messiah would be signaled by a conjunction of planets which appeared to be a "star." The Magi would have known the astronomy and may have even had contact with rabbinic writings to think that Jesus was a new King of the Jews. But this is where the conflict for Mary would surface.

The prevailing thought among rabbis was to shy away from anything suspiciously magical related to astrology. Think about living your life based upon the horoscope in today's newspaper. So at one level Mary's may have been very confused by this visit. On the other hand, she had just heard Simeon say that Jesus would be a light to the Gentiles. The Magi were Gentiles. Could this be a beginning to fulfilling the prophecy she just heard at her baby's dedication? We can't assume that Mary would have immediately accepted their visit as a positive event in her life or that of her son.

Humanly speaking, there isn't a mother on earth who isn't aware of someone else looking at her baby. That look may be negative and the mother becomes protective. But if someone looks adoringly at her child, she's loving it. So Mary has to have also been enamored by this visit of important men who've traveled so great a distance to bring her child gifts. Mary and Joseph were poor. They could increase their income with at least the gold and may even get some money for the incense and myrrh. Mary wouldn't have assigned any great theological meaning to the gifts at this time. There's no way she would have considered the myrrh as a symbol for Jesus' crucifixion and death. Why would she want to? Even though incense is traditionally a symbol for Jesus's divinity, Mary had lots of ways to use it. Mary may have needed it for her eye shadow like Egyptian women at the time. Possibly she viewed it as perfume for Jesus or herself. Given her knowledge of Judaism, she may have wanted to give it to a Zechariah for the altar of incense in the temple. The monetary value of the gold and their financial needs would present Mary with a difficult decision as one who needed the money yet would want to help the temple. Of course, what would the Eastern visitors think if she pawned the gold, used the incense for perfume and saved the myrrh for the burial of a friend or relative? The incense and myrrh were literally "worth their weight in gold."

Mary was conflicted about the visitors and their gifts. Their visit posed more problems than affirmations. The entire city was in a stir and Herod in a panic over their arrival. They brought a message to Herod which threatened his power and authority as the pseudo-Jewish king of Israel. What the Magi meant for good became a huge problem for the city of David and ultimately for Mary just beginning to raise her family. It is not unlikely that the news of Herod's irritation made it to Bethlehem before the knock on Mary's door. Let's assume she knew that her child was the cause of a city-wide problem. Could Mary have recalled once again Simeon's words, "the falling of many." The Magi, even with their gifts, were trouble.

Mary had another question. If the temple leaders had Micah's prophecy memorized so that they could tell a group of pagan visitors Jesus' location, why weren't they at Jesus' manger? The very ones who should be affirming her baby as king were absent. It was Babylonians who recognized Jesus as king. Go figure! Mary no doubt knew about Micah's prophecy as a student of the Law and Prophets, but her thoughts now were more about the possible need to protect her family from the public uproar caused by well-intentioned visitors.

Luke tells us that the astrologers bowed and worshiped Jesus. Not Mary. There was no cultural precedent to worship the mother of a king in Persia or Babylon, and certainly none in Jewish culture.

Bowing before a king occurred in a few instances in Israel's past as an act of respect. However, according to the Law worship was exclusively for Yahweh as stated in the initial commandments. God had a way of getting jealous when people worshiped those "other gods." What these Persians were doing was bringing gifts for a king, not a savior. There is no basis for thinking that the Magi viewed Jesus as the savior of humanity. They bowed out of respect for a king. The only one who realized that Jesus was divine was Mary. Nothing about their gifts conveyed any understanding that Jesus was messiah. Their respect for Mary's baby was limited to his royalty. Culturally, it was what Persians or Babylonians did in front of king. They didn't convert to Judaism as a result of this visit. Nor did they leave Mary's house believing that her toddler was the son of God. Scripture say nothing about their faith.

We can imagine Mary reflecting on the dedication in the temple. How could pagan Magi confirm Simeon's prophecy? But the gifts were so nice. She may have said, "Look how respectful they were to my son." Was her son the cause of Jerusalem's turbulence? Is there any way that her family wouldn't be blamed for riots in the streets? Could this be the sword Simeon was talking about? And Gabriel *did* talk about continuing David's throne? Maybe that's all this was about–astrologers affirming part of the message; just the royalty portion. If so, was Jesus just a king?

How might the Magi visit impacted Mary? What do we learn about her evolving relationship with her son? "Is my baby God or not? Is he the savior of the world or only a king of Israel? How will I ever know for sure?" Let's get into these issues by going back to the very beginning as we conclude this vignette.

Mary had input from an angel, a cousin, shepherds, a devout man, a prophetess, and the Magi as to the identity of her son. Each one spoke or demonstrated their understanding of who Jesus was. One thing we know, there was no consistency among all of these influences where Mary could look back and say with one hundred percent assurance that Jesus was the son of God, a king for David's eternal throne, a light to the Gentiles, glory for Israel and the savior of all humanity. For Mary it had to be like trying to identify an elephant when blindfolded touching its trunk, its side, its tail, and its huge feet.

Gabriel's message was the most comprehensive and it convinced Mary to humbly participate in God's mission for global salvation. Visiting with Elizabeth affirmed her decision to obey and bear the son of God for which she received her cousin's blessing. Recall that Elizabeth was most impressed with Mary's faith to believe that what God had said would come to pass. The shepherds echoed angelic messages of a coming savior bringing peace. Was the conflict currently brewing in Bethlehem God's idea of peace? At Jesus' dedication Mary received a bitter-sweet message from both Simeon and Anna. How would her son be light to the Gentiles and glory to Israel at the same time? Most confusing were Simeon's words about a sword. What did that mean? Finally, we have the Magi returning home by a different route because of Herod. Did Mary even know this? If so, what might her questions have been? Did she anticipate Herod's murder of those twenty or so young male children just so a jealous king could be sure he got the right one–her son? Mary had to be conflicted about her baby's identity. The Magi's visit led to an event Mary could not have anticipated. Nor would she have wanted to. It would result in long trip–another journey she didn't plan. From Simeon's bitter-sweet words to the arrival of these strangers from the east, we continue to experience with Mary the difficulties associated with determining her baby's true identity. Was her baby God? Mary may have had time to ponder this question during an ironic trip to Egypt, of all places, for her son's safety. "Really, God, back to Egypt where we were slaves?"

Chapter 7

Frightened

Matthew 2: 13-31

After the Eastern Magi left, an angel of the Lord appeared to Joseph saying, "Get up and take the child and his mother to Egypt and stay there until I tell you because Herod is going to search for your child to kill him." So during the night they escaped to Egypt and stayed there until Herod died to fulfill Hosea's prophecy that God's son would be called out of Egypt. To be sure he would kill Jesus, Herod gave orders to murder all boys in Bethlehem and its vicinity who were under the age of two. This brutal act reminded Mary of Rachel's weeping over the loss of her children during the exile to Babylon. After Herod died the angel reappeared to Joseph in and said that they could now return. So they went back to Israel. But when Joseph heard that Herod's son became king, he feared going back to Bethlehem in Judea. So through another angelic warning received in a dream, Joseph went to Nazareth a town in Galilee to fulfill the prophetic words that Jesus would be called a Nazarene.

JOSEPH, MARY AND TODDLER Jesus were frightened and running for their lives. Joseph had just learned they needed to leave Bethlehem because Herod was about to kill all boys under two years old. "Not another trip," Mary might have thought. Could she trust her husband's dreams? How many of your dreams do you trust? By now Mary was getting used to God's communication through angels and started packing for another unscheduled trip. How much food would they need? Could she pawn the gold from the Magi for the money they'd need along with way? Why Egypt? Recall that Mary sang her hymn of worship at Elizabeth's house based upon her knowledge of the Torah. She knew that the last time Jews were in Egypt, Moses pleaded with Pharoah to let the Jews out of the country. Why was God telling Joseph to go back there?

Mary also had legitimate questions about a pseudo-king planning to murder boys under two years old just to make sure he killed her son. What was that all about? Again, her thoughts went back to Egypt. The last plague. Passover was the celebration which retold the story of how the angel of death passed over the Jewish homes to save their firstborn sons. Might Mary have thought about the mothers of all those Egyptian babies who were killed? How could she not feel the pain of an Egyptian mother who lost her firstborn son on that fateful night? Couldn't they stay in Bethlehem and just put blood on the doorposts as her ancestors did centuries ago?

When Joseph received a second angelic message to return home, on the trip back he told Mary that Egypt needed to be the location of their security because not only was it safely out of Herod's jurisdiction, but that the messiah would have to "be called out of Egypt" to fulfill a prophecy.

While enduring yet another bumpy ride on a donkey, Mary may have pondered why Israel's prophecies required fulfillment in her life. Hadn't she given up a normal, if poor, existence of a housewife tending the hearth and weaving on a loom? Having dinner on the table for Joseph after his long day making chairs didn't sound so terrible. All that might have been redeemed by re-pondering and re-treasuring those happier thoughts about her calling. She'd remember that knowing her relationship to God as his servant resolved all her previous questions.

Maybe it would do the same again.

But there was another recollection from Israel's tattered history prompted by Herod's insanity. The slaughter of matriarch Rachel's children on their way into exile in Babylon. The same country from which the Magi might have come. Matthew's mention of this event in the nation's life fits with at least the two mass slaughters of children in Israel's history. At that first pass-over, Israel was spared and Egypt wasn't; in the case of Babylon, the Jewish people experienced losses not only within captivity, but also on their journey. Mary may have thought about the irony of finding refuge in a country which had enslaved them. Something to ponder, isn't it?

Mary treasured her faith in God as the one who can do the impossible. Could this be another type of Holy Spirit's presence? Having been frightened throughout this unplanned journey for her son's survival, she was grateful to God for his protection and provision. But there is no way that these events didn't take a toll on her life. At the same time, Mary, continued to grow as a disciple of her own son.

Just when everything seemed to be calming down another angel informed Joseph that even though Herod was dead, his equally dangerous son was now on the throne and they needed to lengthen their trip by seventy miles to live in Nazareth. Can you hear Mary saying, "Here we go again!"

It's amazing how one journey involved so much history and prophecy: that messiah would need to come out of Egypt, that Mary would recall Rachel's loss on her way into captivity, and finally that Jesus would be called a Nazarene. There may not be another person in all of Scripture whose rapidly changing life involved so much prophecy fulfillment. This is yet another part of Mary's uniqueness. She was where the action of God was, whether she realized it at the time or not. While there were women used mightily of God throughout Israel's history, there is no woman who compares to the distinguished life Mary led as Yahweh's humble servant who simply obeyed the Lord.

The statement about Jesus being called a Nazarene, one from Nazareth is a bitter-sweet message. On one hand, this word can mean *branch*, which is a positive reflection on Jesus' messianic status going back to Samuel, the first prophet and continuing with Isaiah. The irony attached to his word is that it can also mean "despised." Mary would later learn that when one of the disciples heard that Jesus as Messiah was from Nazareth he challenged the statement with, "Nazareth, can anything good come from there?" as the Apostle John records in his gospel.

So Mary was directed by God to raise her son in a village with a bad reputation. Nazareth was in the region known as Galilee. Bethlehem was in Judah. It was common knowledge that the Aramaic spoken in Galilee was inferior to that spoken in Judah. Looking ahead, recall that a servant girl outside in the courtyard where Jesus was being tried identified Peter as "one of them" because of his Galilean accent which stuck out like a sore thumb in Jerusalem.

Mary would have known Isaiah's prediction that the messiah would be despised; that is, he'd be a "Nazarene." So we have a play on words which is actually predicted by Israel's prophets.

It's highly likely that later in her life, when she'd have more time to reflect on the implications of this journey, Mary would be able to link Simeon's words about her son being spoken against with God's sending them back to Nazareth to live. There were no mere coincidences in Mary's life. All of it deepened her knowledge of Jesus' identity which evolved throughout her life.

While Jesus was growing wisdom and grace, she was growing spiritually. Can you imagine her reflecting on this frightful trip which saved her son so that he could suffer and die for humanity's salvation? Mary, the mother of God, was truly one of the first pioneers navigating her way with God through the experience of angelic visits and the horrific Herods.

So the newly-returned family settled in Nazareth. This is where Mary would become Jesus' primary educator on his way to become a the son of the commandments. Mary would make sure that Jesus, her son as God incognito, would know the Law that he gave Moses on the top of a mountain centuries before. So she simply acted like any other Jewish mother and brought her son up to be a good Jewish boy. While on a Passover pilgrimage to Jerusalem, Mary would get a powerful lesson in what it would be like to be God's mother.

Chapter 8

Overwhelmed

Luke 2: 41–52

When Jesus was twelve years old, he went with his parents to Jerusalem for the feast of the Passover. Mary and Joseph went home after the feast, but Jesus stayed behind in Jerusalem without his parents' knowledge. They traveled for a whole day before realizing that Jesus wasn't with them. They looked for him among their relatives and friends. When they didn't find him, they traveled for a day back to Jerusalem. It took another day searching Jerusalem before they found Jesus in the temple courts talking with the teachers. Everyone who heard him asking and answering questions was amazed at his knowledge. Mary and Joseph were overwhelmed with joy when they saw him. But his mother said to him, "Son, why have you treated us like this? Your father and I have been anxiously searching for you." Jesus answered, "Why were you searching for me? Didn't you know I had to be in my Father's house?" Mary and Joseph had no idea what he was talking about. Jesus then joined his parents on the journey back to Nazareth. He was an obedient child and grew in wisdom, stature, and in favor with God and all others. Mary treasured all these things in her heart.

Mary Gave God a Body

ONE REASON JESUS AMAZED the temple scholars and teachers of the Law in the temple was that he had an excellent teacher. Mary. The primary educator of the rituals and traditions in a Jewish home was the mother. Mary taught Jesus that the *mezuzah* on their doorpost was a scroll inscribed with Deuteronomy 6: 4–9 stating the *Shema* "Hear, O Israel, the Lord our God, the Lord is one. Love the Lord your God with all your heart, soul and strength. These commandments I give you today are to be upon your hearts. Write them on the doorposts of your houses." Jesus would quote this often in his ministry. He memorized it from his childhood. Jesus would light the seven candles of the *menora* to remember when Yahweh gave Moses instructions to design a candlestick for the tabernacle to represent that Israel was to reflect the glory of the Lord by living obedient lives. Mary taught her son about Esther's role in saving the nation celebrated in *Purim*, New Year's day called *Rosh Hashana*, *Yom Kippur* the day of atonement and how to make the booths for *Sukkoth* remembering to work toward renewing the earth. Jesus' knowledge as son of the commandments came from his mother and did not rely solely on his divinity. Temple leaders were used to bright Jewish boys well versed in the faith. However, this event had to be unique given the unusual amazement by the temple scholars at Jesus' profound questions and insightful answers. This Jewish boy was exceptional and all marveled at his wisdom. This was his divinity coming out.

As influential as Mary was in Jesus' Jewish education, this story isn't about that. This vignette is about how Mary's apparent negligence as a mother deepened her knowledge of who her son really was. It wouldn't be the only time tension in their relationship ended well.

She lost track of her child for an entire day and didn't find him for three days. Before getting into it, I would ask any mother this question: How much time would it take before you're panicked about not knowing the whereabouts of your child? One minute? 10 minutes? An hour? Would it ever last for an entire day? I can't imagine any mother in any culture who would allow an entire day to go by before beginning to look for her child?

One common justification for Mary's mistake is that because caravans included close family and friends, a parent could be sure their child was with family when not by her side. There is no research about caravans and parents which would justify such an explanation. What's clear from this story is that Mary was lost, not her son. If we read the conversation closely between Jesus and his mother once he's found, we'll discover whose fault it was that Mary and her child weren't together. It's surprising to me after looking at several sources on this topic how Mary is let off the hook by commentaries and biblical scholars. No one allows Mary to be human. It seems that she must always come out pure and right–all the time. Mary must always appear inhumanly perfect. To repeat: one theme of this book is that the mother of God was human.

Luke begins the Luke begins the problematic portion of the pilgrimage, not with a statement about Mary, but about Jesus. He never left the temple with his parents. How often has that happened to any parents? But why did Jesus remain in the temple? Did he rebel against his mother wanting to be an independent twelve-year-old; after all, he was a son of the commandments.

Jesus remained in the temple because he felt at home. He was in his father's house. He never felt lost in this story. Mary was lost without him. Parenthetically, anyone who leaves Jesus behind soon discovers how lost they really are and need God back in their life.

If Jesus' siblings were among those in the caravan, I wonder how they would have felt watching their mother in a panic about not knowing where their brother was? This couldn't have added to their security as her children. They had to be upset as well. Where was their brother? Why did mom and dad allow this to happen? What if they did this to us?

After three days, Mary and Joseph finally found Jesus in the temple with the temple scholars and teachers of the Law. He was wholeheartedly engaged in deeply theological conversation asking good questions. He impressed the elders. They were probably more impressed with his answers to questions they posed. We need to view Jesus' time in the temple as the give and take of questions and answers which characterized how learning took place between Jewish teachers and students.

Mary's emotions were mixed when she found her son. She's relieved and exasperated at the same time. A religious Mary would have said, "Jesus, of course, you left your mother because you had to do God's work in the temple, I completely understand." Never.

Or, "I didn't miss you for a minute, I know you are God and you have higher priorities than obeying your parents." No way. Luke has Mary saying, "How could you do this to us?" A perfectly normal response by a panicked, yet relieved mother.

Jesus asked her two questions. "Why were you searching for me?" and "Didn't you know that I needed to do the things of my Father?" Those things at this time meant for him to be in his Father's house engaged in learning and discussing his faith. He wasn't lost. He was at home.

Jesus is never lost. We are. Mary and Joseph were. To be fair, we've been saying all along that Mary's grasp of her son's identity as the son of God evolved with just about every encounter with him. We've seen this in earlier events and we'll take note of it later as well. Jesus implies that his mother should have known where he'd be if not with her.

Humanly speaking Jesus is cutting the apron strings; it's the beginning of his adolescent crisis. Few mothers are ready for their kids to go through this and it's a difficult time in any family. Note that Jesus doesn't admit to having done anything wrong to his mother.

He puts it back on her. He was fine. She was panicked and started searching for someone who wasn't lost. Jesus was beginning to educate his teacher about who he was. Throughout all the stories involving Mary and Jesus, the key questions are "What did Mary know about Jesus?" and "When did she know it?" Mary taught Jesus Jewish traditions; Jesus taught her about God.

In his ministry, the discrepancy between religious tradition and one's relationship with God characterized the most frequent tension between Jesus and religious leaders. Was it possibly these same teachers of the law in the temple that day who gave Jesus the most grief during his time on earth.

Jesus' last question indicated that he needed to be in his father's house. Think about how Joseph might have felt after hearing this. Wasn't his father's business carpentry?

Wasn't Joseph training his son to take over the family business as a carpenter? Joseph had to be as confused as Mary during this entire event. They simply had no idea what he was talking about. Yet, this story ends on a positive note, How does this encounter between Mary and Jesus have a good ending? Note that once again, Mary ended up treasuring all these things in her heart. The last time Luke used this phrase was right after Mary had given birth. She had both pre-birth and post-birth events over which to ponder–Gabriel, Elizabeth and Zechariah, John the Baptizer, shepherds, a chorus of angels singing about her baby, and mostly affirming words from Simeon and Anna in the temple. But now as Jesus was growing up, things weren't always so positive. The Passover pilgrimage was the first event of many that Mary would experience showing her how God can make lemonade out of lemons. That is, that God may take an apparently difficult situation and redeem it.

Even through difficult encounters with Jesus, Mary's belief in her son's divinity grew.

Though upset with him, she overheard his intelligent conversations with Jewish scholars of the Hebrew sacred scriptures–the law, psalms and prophets. She may had heard some things she had taught him. But that day in the temple, she heard things come out of Jesus' mouth which were new to her. How could her son have known all these good questions and excellent answers if he weren't the son of the Most High destined to sit on David's throne for all eternity? Though appearing disobedient, Mary's son willingly joined and stayed with them for the entire trip home and grew in grace and in favor with all people.

This was the first post-birth event involving Mary and Jesus we find selected from the oral tradition for the canon of holy scripture. It reveals both Jesus' humanity as an adolescent as well as Mary's humanity as a mother. Mary came out of this awkward encounter with her son realizing a lot about his divinity; possibly more than in any other previous bitter-sweet event.

This is the last recorded story about Jesus' childhood in the Scriptures. Biblical authors go from an adolescent Jesus right into his ministry as a thirty-year-old man. We now get into the familiar story of the Cana wedding

Chapter 9

Pushy

John 2: 1–11

One day Mary, Jesus and his disciples attended a wedding in Cana. When Mary saw that they had run out of wine, she said to Jesus, "They have no more wine." Jesus replied, "Woman, how is that any concern of yours or mine? My hour has not yet come." Mary said to the servants, "Do whatever he tells you." Nearby stood six stone jars used for Jewish purification rites. Jesus said to the servants, "Fill the jars with water." They filled them to the brim. Then he told them, "Now draw some out and take it to the master of the banquet." So they did. The master tasted it but did not know that the water had been turned to wine nor did he realize where it come from, even though the disciples did. So he called the bridegroom aside and said, "Everyone usually brings out the choice wine first and then serves the cheaper wine only after the guests are drunk. But you have saved the best for last." This first sign of Jesus' glory in Cana caused his disciples to put their faith in him.

WE ALL WISH WE knew more about Jesus' life from age twelve to thirty. There's simply no data from the biblical witness or other sources about his life during these years. We ended the last chapter with a general statement of his physical, mental, and spiritual growth. Did Jesus ever laugh? Can we imagine him sitting at Mary's feet for yet another lesson from the Torah? One thing we *do* read in all the gospels is the central role of the temple in his life. He went there at age eight for his dedication. Four years later he's back at the temple discussing the Hebrew Scriptures with Jewish scholars. Later, we see him creating a scene in the temple by turning over tables of merchandise which desecrated God's house. In this vignette, we get into the first recorded event of Jesus' ministry. It's now outside the temple that Jesus begins to minister.

The abiding question threaded throughout this book is this: What would have been any ordinary mother's reaction to her child in a similar event? We do know *this* from the Scripture–Mary's experiences with her son were bitter-sweet. At the dedication, she heard words about Jesus which affirmed his deity along with a "sword which would pierce her heart." During the Passover pilgrimage, she lost her son only to hear from him that she should have known where he'd be. Here, we find Jesus challenging his Mary's attempt to advance his cause. In each awkward interaction, Mary's knowledge of Jesus' divinity gradually grew. From here on out, such events spiral downward ending at that crucial event for humanity's salvation–the cross. It would be the lowest point in Mary's life.

Cana was only a few miles from Nazareth. The feast-reception of a wedding might last for days. We have Jesus, his brothers, his mother and disciples at the feast. The best hospitality for all invited guests would be expected which explains the embarassing situation of running out of wine. The Apostle John wasn't concerned about protocol at a first century Jewish wedding. Nor is his only reason even to announce Jesus' first miracle. This event is significant for the way it advances ongoing knowledge of her son's true identity. Each mother-son event presented Mary with an opportunity to gradually determine that Jesus was really God. But the wedding at Cana also indicates Jesus detachment from Mary as a young man beginning to carve out his life without his mother. The bitter part for Mary is the respectful greeting yet abrupt response suggesting that the hospitality for someone else's wedding is not their responsibility. He will decide when his ministry should begin. Given the traditional confusion over Jesus' use of *Woman*, we note that John has Jesus using the same word to his mother from the cross; hardly a time when he would have been rude. What begins in the temple at age twelve is continued now. Jesus wants to be on his own. As we'll observe, future events will assure us that no co-dependence characterized this mother-son relationship. Jesus' sense of security as a person sent the message that he no longer needed his mother. Jesus was disconnecting from Mary who, like any mother, struggled with her child's independence. His ultimate disconnect from her occurs at the cross.

That said, the dialogue Jesus has with Mary is not cut and dry. Jesus is also in transition in his relationship with Mary. She doesn't give up. She's still his mother. Mary knows how she'd feel if this were a wedding for one of her children. She's pushy. Her response to those going around filling the glasses of wine for the guests is prophetic: "Do whatever he tells you." This is a classic statement by a mother which overrides her child's thinking and behavior. Mary may have thought, "I don't care what he said, he doesn't know how important it is that guests get the best care at a wedding, I'll just pretend I didn't hear him." This puts the servers in the middle of a Mary-Jesus conflict. Word about this up-and-coming rabbi has gotten around. They'd run the risk of violating his desires; after all, who wants to challenge a rabbi? At the same time, Mary is his mother; she's got something to say about all this as well. To whom should they listen?

We suggest that this key event is where Mary knows that her son is the messiah.. It is surely a huge turning point in her relationship with Jesus. Mary has here decided that her son really is who Gabriel, Elizabeth, shepherds, singing angels, Simeon, Anna, and foreign star-gazers said he was. Mary now believes beyond the shadow of a doubt that her thirty-three-year old son is God.

What's remarkable is that Jesus changes his mind. What was he thinking? He obeys Mary and performs a miracle. There is no way this isn't a miracle. Because the helpers filled those huge earthen jars right up the brim, there was no room to add anything to the water. The molecular structure of the liquid changed from only hydrogen and oxygen to something which included that of fermented grapes. Not only that, this new-and-improved wine altered traditional practice at a wedding. The best was saved for last. And people noticed. The Cana wedding anticipates how Jesus consistently stood ordinary ways of thinking upside down. To restate, John never tells his readers why Jesus changed his mind. We can only speculate that he may not have fully worked out his complete independence. He heard his mother's teaching voice just like we continue to "hear" the voices of our parents. Mary's guiding words from his childhood were still in his head. It's the last recorded time Mary said anything to Jesus. Note that Mary doesn't tell Jesus to change the water to wine; that's *his* way of solving the problem. Mary talks to the servers. They listen to her. Whether Jesus overheard her or not is only speculation. Finally, John mentions how this first miracle changed the minds of fishermen who for the first time begin to trust Jesus.

John never indicates the impact this miracle had upon Mary. He doesn't need to. Had she any doubt about Jesus' ability to perform a miracle, she would have sent the servants to the store to get more cheap wine. But Mary sees what's going on here. Her son is not only performing a miracle as a sign of his divinity to the Jewish community; it also anticipates his method to change ordinary custom and religion into radical kingdom thinking. The best wine was served toward the tail end of the reception. Jesus would later say, "The first shall be last." Mary's son would replace common religion with loving God and neighbor.

So an apparently rude conversation with her son over control displays Mary's trust in Jesus. Conflict is turned into faith. Doubt becomes obedience. The mother of God modelswhat it means to be a disciple. Jesus' radical methods in this first recorded event of his adult ministry come to light. Our next vignette, however, turns the tables on Mary; for herson radically changes the concept of motherhood.

Chapter 10

Insulted

Matthew 12: 46–50; Mark 3: 31–35; Luke 8: 19–21

One day Jesus was in a house teaching about Satan called Beelzebub, the prince of demons. The Pharisees accused Jesus of healing demon-possessed people in the name of the devil. Then they challenged him to perform a spectacular miracle in the sky to prove he was the Messiah. The word got back to Mary and his brothers that people were accusing Jesus of being out of his mind. She went to the house with her sons where he was teaching, but couldn't get in because of the crowd so they stood outside waiting to speak with him. Someone told Jesus that his mother and brothers were at the door. Jesus replied, "Who is my mother, and who are my brothers?" Then, pointing to his disciples, he said, "Here are my mother and my brothers. For whoever hears God's word, puts it into practice and does my heavenly Father's will is my brother, sister, and mother."

ONLY THE PRE-BIRTH EVENTS about her son were positive for Mary. Mary's relationship with Jesus began a downward spiral with the dedication in the temple right up to the event we discuss now–Mary's rescue mission to spare Jesus' bullying by local religious leaders. Word had gotten to Mary that while Jesus was in a home teaching about Satan, he was being accused of doing his ministry of healing with appeals to demonic power. Mary showed up at this location with her sons and stood at the door requesting to speak with him. Because it was so crowded they were unable to see Jesus face to face. As you just read above, word got to Jesus that his mother and brothers were at the door.

Before getting into the story, it's important to note that this is the only Mary-Jesus encounter that all three synoptic gospel authors record. One reason may be that this event, short of the dialogue at the cross, represents the most difficult conflict for Mary. To review her life, Mary's pre-birth announcements and conversations offered her an increasingly positive experience about becoming the mother of God. Gabriel's initial seemingly impossible words ended up resolved through Mary's understanding of her relationship with God. He could do apparently impossible things like supernaturally impregnating a human being resulting in mysterious person with two natures–divine and human. Needing to tell somebody about this unplanned pregnancy, Mary rushed to Elizabeth and received a most-needed affirmation that she would be blessed as the mother of God's son. Ecstatically, Mary sang a substantive praise song extolling Jehovah for who he is and what's he's done both for her, for people in need, for Abraham, and for the nation of Israel. The height of Mary's fulfilling experience of motherhood occurred, as it does for any mother, at the birth of her son including choirs of angels and lowly shepherds. But the birth of Jesus would be her last purely positive encounter and experience related to her unique calling.

From Simeon's painfully obscure words about a sword, about causing the falling of many and being spoken against, to scolding Jesus for lagging behind on the trip home from Passover and to Jesus' challenge to her at the Cana wedding and now this apparent rebuff by not even coming to the door to talk to his own mother– all these events may have raised the question in her mind, "Where did I go wrong?" At best, Mary may have pondered, not all the wonderful things from the past, but self-doubt. At worst, there's the likelihood that Mary was insulted not only by Jesus' refusal to come to the door, but also his re-definition of motherhood with the question, "Who is my mother?" When Mary got word about this she could have easily thought that the messenger got it wrong, for *her* son would *never* say such a thing. She may have mulled, "Didn't I give this child birth? Didn't this boy come from my flesh?"

Mary may have recalled the past conflicts between her and Jesus. Somehow all of them achieved some degree of resolution. The awkward and strained conversations were resolved as she pondered and treasured the positive messages from the past about her son. All the potentially embarrassing debates Jesus had with the temple and synagogue leaders and all the risks involved in becoming impure by touching lepers and socializing with tax collectors–all these, while awkward and shameful, never challenged her motherhood. But this question, "Who is my mother?" had to be a gut punch to Mary. It was not only the question, but also its answer that she found hurtful.

Jesus re-defined motherhood to include men. How did this comport with Jewish tradition holding high the feminine gender for giving birth and nurturing children in the faith? Was Jesus into identity politics? Men? Women? Brothers? Sisters? Mothers? How could all these be his mother? Wasn't Jesus being inclusive? We can be sure that Mary did not resolve this insult to her motherhood by interpreting Jesus' words theologically. That would come later as she took her place in the church. Both Jesus' question and answer had to have hurt Mary deeply.

Looking back through a theological lens at this event, we know that New Testament apostles wrote about the church as the family of God and a household of faith. But put yourself in Mary's position. Would you be thinking theologically right now with her on that doorstep? It what sense could Mary possibly find comfort in hearing that a future disciple named Nathaniel was Jesus' mother? Did he ever change Jesus' diapers?

To be fair Scripture never says that Jesus *intended* to hurt his mother's feelings. Recall that Jesus always treated his mother with respect. Nothing about what he said to Mary in the temple while talking with the religious leaders after Passover was rude.

If anything, Mary may have had to walk back her scolding. Jesus went home to be an obedient child. He could have felt that he had reason to rebel on being rebuked by his mother for simply doing God's will.

No gospel author attempts a resolution to this conflicted situation with Mary with her sons at the door. We don't have Mary pondering and treasuring anything in her heart as a result of this awkward encounter. We see her waiting impatiently to hear from her son. We see Jesus using her arrival at the door as a teachable moment about discipleship.

Every encounter between Mary and Jesus informs a biblical definition of the church. We anticipate such a conversation here since it fits future statements from New Testament apostles about the church. Mary gave God the body he needed to become head of the church on earth. This is simply another way to underline the theme of this book. From an anthropology of Mary's life, we see an emergent theology of the church. While her role begins and ends with biology, without it the Word does not become flesh as the Apostle John would write. Mary's son will become the head of the church. She will merely become a mother in the church, not the Mother of the Church. This distinction is a critical teaching from Mary's life. Everything about Mary forms the basis for something far more important than she. It's all about Christ and the church. For all that's recorded about Mary has the makings for a theology of Jesus Christ traditionally known as Christology. What is true about the church must be true about Christ. What is true about Christ must be true about the church. More on this in the Conclusion.

In this chapter we've spanned the wide gap of an insulted mother at a door concluding with a definition of the church. We've attempted to portray a human Mary, not a teflon mother who is impervious to feeling hurt. That said, we've noted that Jesus did not mean to offend his mother, but used this awkward incident as a teaching moment. Understandably, these words from her son had to have hurt her deeply. As difficult as this incident was for

Insulted

Mary, there is no way she could anticipate the deep wound she'd experience during the last time she would see her son. At the cross.

Chapter 11

Devastated

John 19: 25–27

Near the cross of Jesus stood his mother, his mother's sister, Mary the wife of Clopas, and Mary Magdalene. When Jesus saw his mother there and the disciple whom he loved standing nearby, he said to his mother, "Woman, here is your son," and to the disciple, "Here is your mother." From that time on, this disciple took her into his home.

John names four people other than himself standing at the foot of Jesus' cross. Jesus' mother Mary, her sister [who is Salome, John's mother making Jesus and John first cousins], Mary the wife of Clopas and Mary Magdalene, the first person to whom Jesus would appear after rising from the dead. The theme of this chapter is the church. The church begins at the cross where Jesus is present with his mother and disciples. Who Jesus defined as "mother, brother and sister" from the last chapter now takes initial shape by forming a new community of human beings centered around the cross. No one is thinking theologically here. Mary is too devastated to recall her last recorded event at the door of a house where she didn't even get to speak to her son. She's too grieved to speak to anyone. John is there by her side ready to catch her if she faints looking at her child die. As horrific as all this is for him, Jesus thinks of others. He's caring for his mother and close friend John while giving his life to save humanity. So our focus at the cross is the formation of the church with Mary of Nazareth, John, her nephew and Jesus forming a human trinity of persons about to enter into a radically new relationship. Simultaneously, we don't forget how horrific this scene is for Mary.

Notice who isn't standing at the foot of the cross. Where are the men? Where are Jesus' brothers? They are not at the cross because they have not been followers of their brother. In fact, they've probably been ashamed of Jesus. The absence of the male disciples is more difficult to explain. Some would say they feared being arrested themselves so they hid. Others say they were too embarrassed at the death of their failed leader. Not one of them viewed Jesus' death as the major event to save the world. No disciple of Jesus was thinking theologically at his death. They were scared and deflated. Their leader was dead and he looked really bad doing it as a crucified criminal. There's no reason to believe that any disciple of Jesus, including John, linked the Last Supper with the cross. There is no record that Jesus' "This is my body for you" from their last meal together was recognized as being fulfilled by Jesus' death. The only theologian at the foot of the cross was a Roman centurion who acknowledged this criminal as the son of God.

Jesus' redefinition of the family as those who do his father's will is actualized at the cross. Biology is no longer a criterion for "being family." Note that Jesus doesn't emphasize blood line in his words either to Mary or John. All three of them are related by blood. All three of them realize the role of being Jewish family. Yet, Jesus stands culture on its head. He's more interested in launching a new humanity–a community of mothers, sisters and brothers no longer only identified by race, gender or socio-economic status. Spiritually, the common denominator of this new community would be a personal relationship with Jesus himself evidenced by loving God and neighbor.

It would be naïve to suggest that Jesus' new definition dismantling cultural norms comes about without consequences.

When Mary and John hear his words uniting them across biological boundaries, they must have thought about their roots as Jews. First, the Jewish concept of family provided them with status. To be a child of Abraham was to be a cut above all non-Jews. After all, they were God's chosen. Yahweh was in a special covenant relationship with Israel compared with all other nations. Second, if you were part of a Jewish family you were assured a place in the kingdom of God. The Jewish family offered one salvation; you're standing with God depended upon your Jewish religion. Third, the Jewish family provided one with a sense of security. To reject traditional cultural norms to become a Jesus-follower would have serious consequences. It would cost something to be Jesus' disciple.

Mary wasn't pondering the impact of her son's rearrangement of the family. She was standing there losing a son. Jesus said, "Woman, here is your son." She knew her son was there–dying on a cross. What other son mattered? Jesus was caring for his widowed mother on the day she was about to lose her first child. The cross is the first place and time Scripture indicates that Jesus cared for his mother. He wanted to die being assured that she would be loved. So John his cousin, not Jesus' brothers, is asked to "adopt" Mary as his "mother." We can be sure that John's account of this scene is accurate since he was there. John took her to his home.

Recall the significance of "taking Mary home" going back to Joseph. The true test of marriage was that a husband would provide for his wife by taking her home as the angel told Joseph to do. This would be the second time someone would care for her in this way. The first time was to authenticate her marriage to avoid shame; this second time had a twofold purpose. First, Jesus would die assured of his mother's care by his closest friend and wouldn't have to rely on his brothers; second, this new Mary-John relationship foreshadowed the new humanity, the church, which Jesus came to establish. John followed his new mother's advice from the Cana wedding and did what Jesus said. Here we have Jesus turning cultural norms on their head. The rightful care-givers for Mary would have been her sons. They didn't assume this role for their own mother. But this fits with Jesus' new definition of family. Jewish cultural tradition became secondary. We speculate that as Mary progressed through the grieving process, she entered into a motherly relationship with John which had to include long conversations about Jesus' life. No other gospel author had this advantage. Along with the Spirit's inspiration, the accuracy of John's gospel is a function of his close relationship with Mary, the mother of God. Can you see him taking notes as Mary tells her story?

Mary is the only woman in history who fulfilled both definitions of motherhood–biological and spiritual. Biologically, she was Jesus of Nazareth's mother for thirty-three years. She was an ordinary mother of an extraordinary child. Throughout this book we've spoken of the human Mary. We've talked about how her knowledge of her son's the true identity was gradual, often characterized by conflict. As a good mother, Mary always knew the human needs of her child. Ironically, Mary became Jesus' disciple, a spiritual mother, before she became Jesus' mother. She obeyed God by having his son. God's son in heaven would become Mary's son on earth. This is why we bless her as the first disciple of the church. That's also why even though she may have been insulted when Jesus introduced his new idea of motherhood, she was already qualified as a disciple. But Mary isn't pondering any theology now. Standing at the foot of the cross, she was devastated as any mother would be. Any thoughts of her being a "spiritual" mother in the church would come much later. Not today.

Mary had to be pondering that "sword" Simeon talked about on that bitter-sweet day in the temple. "Is this what he meant?" she may have thought. A spear thrust into her son's side resulted in an emotional cut on her heart. "Was this that sword which would pierce your heart also?" The piercing of Nazareth's gossip she could handle. She had help from Elizabeth. The incessant criticism from the temple leaders was like getting stabbed in the back. But she could temper her feelings by observing how well her son handled them. All of these "swords" came to mind. So this is what Simeon meant.

This last day that Mary would see Jesus is tragic for her. There is no softening the negative impact of her watching her son die a cruel death. Mary's endures the bewildering emotion of losing and gaining a son on the same day. There is no reason to believe that going home with John would replace the loss of her baby. Any attempt to spiritualize or romanticize this day in Mary's life is inhumane. Mary wasn't singing "Jesus keep me near the cross" today. She wanted to be anywhere else but here. Mary was in no shape to look at her son on that cross and see him as her savior and Lord. She was devastated. There is no record that Mary visited Jesus' tomb with spices. She was in too much grief and probably refused to be comforted. Can you blame her? But this scene doesn't have the last word for her.

The next place we find Mary is with her family in church. It will be the last time she's mentioned in Scripture. It's the first explicit statement of the church. Mary is praying with the new community composed of her sisters and brothers in Christ.

Chapter 12

Restored

Acts 1: 12-14

After Jesus ascended to heaven the disciples met together for prayer, along with the women, Mary the mother of Jesus and her sons.

MUCH OCCURRED IN THE forty days from Jesus' resurrection to this prayer meeting where Mary's relationship with Jesus is restored. We left Mary at the cross in the last chapter. She never went to the tomb. Jesus never appeared to her after coming back to life. Mary went home with John and continued grieving the loss of her child. She no doubt returned to her routine milling the grain for bread, tending the hearth and working the loom just like any Mediterranean housewife would. She sought no special honor or recognition. She may have recalled singing the *Magnificat,* "All generations will call her blessed." She may have also recalled Jesus' response to a woman who said, "Blessed is the womb that bore you and the breasts that nursed you!" with "Blessed rather are those who hear the word of God and obey it." That is, Jesus simply restated his redefinition of an ordinary disciple with no reference to Mary. For the second time.

Mary, now about forty eight years old, is with the disciples in that upper room where the task at hand is to replace Judas. Mary watches with great interest as the dice are rolled and Matthias is selected as a witness to the resurrected Messiah. She never went to Jesus' empty tomb nor was she present when he ascended as far as we know. She simply shows up in the church as disciple. Later she would hear about how the church, the body of Christ. It's the closest she'd ever get to "seeing" her son again. Of course, here his body is not flesh, but spirit. The new community, the church, has taken the place of Jesus' physical body on earth. Mary is simply a participant in the church life along with everyone else. She's praying to her son. She's studying the word in community with both women and men. She's singing praises to God with other brothers, sisters and mothers just like she did during her visit with Elizabeth. Mary is an excellent model of what it means worship God.

The matter-of-fact way in which Luke refers to Mary suggests that she simply takes her place as one of the one hundred twenty originals who launched the church in prayer. This same group would be at the Jewish Pentecost celebration when God chooses to give the Holy Spirit to the entire church. Mary receives the Holy Spirit along with everyone else. But she's already modeled this supernatural event when the Holy Spirit came upon her resulting in Jesus' birth. He had overshadowed her to conceive Jesus. Mary had already been filled with the Holy Spirit in a way no one else would ever experience. Just as she was there at the beginning of the new humanity at the foot of the cross, Mary is present as the church receives its power to take the good news of Jesus' death and resurrection to the world. Can you hear her saying, "I've been there before, let me tell you about my experience with the Holy Spirit." I suspect that the humility with which Mary accepted Gabriel's message continued to characterize her spirituality as a member of the early church. What she earlier pondered, she spoke about in church.

She was a mother in the church, not the Mother of the Church. She notices a radical change in the informality of this new community. Women are sitting *with* the men. It doesn't seem to matter. What matters is a sense of shared community. The binding factor is not gender, but the worship of Jesus of Nazareth, the son of the Most High, who has returned from the dead. Mary's son.

She finds other women, other "Elizabeths," to whom she tells her story from beginning to end. These women had to be amazed at her conversation with angel Gabriel. Were they taken back by Jesus' redefining of the family? Is it still Jewish? Mary's not sure what to say but she recalls Jesus' theme about being family means hearing and doing the will of Jehovah. As Mary tells and retells her story, she feels her grief gradually lifting. Participating in this community is a healing experience. It helps her process her loss. She's being restored back to emotional health and life. She sees herself in community with lots of sisters, mothers and brothers. She's with her sons plus an entirely unanticipated family of friends. No longer would she need to face the burdens of life alone.

Mary begins to connect the dots. She didn't attend that last celebration of Passover, a transition to the Lord's Supper, where her son said, "This is my body, this is my blood." She was at the cross, but unable to see its relationship to the Lord's Supper. She wasn't at the empty tomb. She may have been at Jesus' ascension. Sitting in church she may have begun to see how all the events in her life were starting to add up. She gave Jesus his body. He says bread and wine are his body and blood. His bodily death, bodily resurrection, and visible ascension fit into a larger scheme of world redemption. Peter now proclaims forgiveness in relationship with her son. Mary gets it. But there's more.

Mary would have been between seventy and seventy five years old when the Apostle Paul spoke about the new humanity as the body of Christ in his Corinthian and Ephesian letters. The body of Christ. Let's assume that Mary heard about this new way of speaking about this early community of believers as the living body of Jesus Christ. "I gave him his body. Now this great missionary is naming the church after my son calling it the body of Christ. Not only that, he's even referred to the human body as the temple of the Holy Spirit. Was my body such a temple at his birth? Wasn't I filled with the Holy Spirit when overshadowed by the glory of

God which used to hover over the tabernacle? Could this be God's way of giving my son back to me? Wow! At the beginning, his body was in mine. Now I'm in his! I'm reborn in the womb of my son's body in a radical redefinition of conception. Didn't I hear about his conversation with Nicodemus who struggled with this idea of being born again? Is this what my son was talking about? Have I been born again?"

Are the above words recorded in the gospels? No. Speculation as to what Mary might have thought over time? Yes. Reasonable historical fiction? Another "Yes." But however much of a stretch you may think of these above thoughts about the church, the emerging theology of the church combined with a growing awareness of the Holy Spirit supports Mary's possible thinking. She's a theologian. She's constructing an idea about her new community from both the word of God and her unique experience as Jesus' mother. Here Mary is restored as she discovers that all the bittersweet events in her life are summed up in the church. Finally, it all starts to make perfect sense.

Mary will spend the rest of her life with her risen son in the mysterious community of his body, the church. Mary was that special humble servant God chose to usher the son of God to earth as a baby. She taught him the Torah. He knew answers to teachers of the synagogue by sitting at his mother's feet. Her pain and pondering over the past thirty-three years ended well.

At this point, we're at a place where anthropology gives way to interpretation. We now focus our attention to the theological implications surrounding Mary's unique life as an ordinary woman called to do extraordinary things. We conclude by focusing on one of the greatest doctrines of the Christian church called the incarnation.

Conclusion

JESUS' BIRTH WAS SCANDALOUS not religious. Mary of Nazareth was a least likely choice to usher messiah into the world. Our objective was to present a human Mary, not a porcelain figurine with a halo created in the image of religion. Given that good anthropology spawns good theology, we portrayed Mary as an ordinary woman who did extraordinary things for God. We've claimed no more for Mary than she claimed for herself; that is, that all generations would call her blessed. We defined blessed as that special grace from God which empowers someone to fulfill God's mission. Blessed in no way implies that Mary was divine.

Mary was a sinner like the rest of us. The Holy Spirit came over her as a virgin and she found herself pregnant with the son of the Most High. Mary delivered her baby among animals using their feeding trough as a crib. Only shepherds and astrologers visited her son in his early childhood. Jesus soiled himself, got hungry and cried when he was tired. Mary breast-fed the son of God. After giving birth to Jesus, Joseph and Mary had other children and raised their family in a tiny village called Nazareth. As a responsible Jewish mother, Mary told the second person of the Trinity stories from the Torah and the prophets. Jesus was truly a son of the commandments.

Mary experienced the moods and emotions common to any human being. She was a young woman, wife, and mother. As a humble servant of God her fears gave way to peaceful obedience. Mary was exasperated with her twelve-year-old boy, pushy when he started his work, insulted when he shunned her, and was devastated as she watched him slowly die on a cross. She never went to Jesus' tomb at his burial or his resurrection. Jesus never appeared to his mother after he rose from the dead. Mary pondered and treasured all the good and bad in her heart. The highest point of her life was Jesus' birth; the lowest point, his cruel crucifixion.

If you've read this far, you may have been challenged to rethink your view of Mary. Like me, your faith may have been enriched by this strong and brave Spirit-filled woman as a model disciple. Mary was the first person to claim Jesus Christ as her Savior. We now move from Mary's humanity to the theological implications of her relationship with Jesus.

We said that the over-arching theological concept of this book is the incarnation. Literally, "the enfleshing of God." No other world religion claims such a concept. Grace, prophecy and the church are vitally linked to and originate from the incarnation.

Grace may be defined as undeserved favor from God. Gabriel begins by telling Mary she's found favor with God. The Holy Spirit graciously overshadowed Mary with his presence resulting in a supernatural conception. God was the agent; her virginity was the process. The result of this combined agency and process was a Jewish baby boy named Yeshua in Hebrew and Jesus in Latin.

The theology associated with Jesus' arrival is not the virgin birth. The overshadowing of the Holy Spirit is. Mary's virginity is anthropological. It describes only her, not God. A virginal conception does not make God necessary. Mary's virginity requires only that no male sperm fertilized one of Mary's eggs. The Holy Spirit mysteriously "fertilized" one of Mary's eggs. Mary is solely responsible for Jesus' humanity. The Holy Spirit is solely responsible for Jesus' divinity. Mary contributed nothing to Jesus' deity. The Holy Spirit contributed nothing to Jesus' humanity. The coming upon Mary by the Holy Spirit resulting in baby Jesus is a statement of Christology, not Mariology. To repeat, this book claims no theology of Mary. Rather, what's significant is that without Mary, the Apostle John, her inherited son, could not have written, "The Word became flesh."

Conclusion

The only aspect of Jesus' birth which makes God necessary is the mystery of the Holy Spirit. For example, the Holy Spirit could have overshadowed a middle-aged married woman with four kids. Her fifth pregnancy could have been just as supernatural as Mary's. No doubt to her husband's great surprise as well as hers. Since all things are possible with God, He could have chosen this process. The agent would have still been the Holy Spirit. Instead of to a virgin, a supernatural conception would have occurred in the body of a woman with four children. Virginity isn't the issue; the supernatural agent is. Who results from the pregnancy is more important than the process God may have chosen, since all things are possible with God.

No later New Testament author ever mentions the virgin birth of Jesus Christ. One of the Apostle Paul's letters simply states that Jesus was "born of a woman." Not until the second century Apostles' Creed is there any formal statement about Mary's virginity. By that time the Christian church had been up and running for about a century. Note that before the statement about Mary's virginity in the Creed is the theological claim, "conceived by the Holy Spirit." That Jesus Christ is one person with two natures is what's really important; the process that got him there is secondary. It's really all about *who* Jesus is, not so much *how* he got here.

Because Mary found favor with [was graced by] God, the Holy Spirit overshadowed her. Mary's purity was not a condition for her maternity. Mary possessed no qualifications to be the mother of God. Mary had no merits earning her a right to do what she did. Jesus was her savior because of his merits, not hers. No one before or after her has played so special a role in God's presence on earth. God chose not to accomplish his mission on earth without her. Mary gave God the body he needed to save the world.

Just as God graced Mary, He has also graced us in the life, death and resurrection of Jesus Christ. The Apostle Paul reminds the church that grace has saved us; nothing we could have done has earned our salvation. Jesus Christ plus zero is necessary and sufficient to forgive sinners like us. Not by anything we can do, but only because of God's mercy can we enjoy a personal relationship with Jesus Christ. The mystery of God's grace to Mary is the same for our salvation. What I don't understand, I gladly receive as a gracious gift from God; that is, his daily presence making me his only destination on the journey through life.

Prophecy is a second core theological concept associated with Mary. Prophecy is both proclaimed and fulfilled in Mary's lifetime.. Prophecy may be the forth-telling of God's word or a foretelling of future events. Recall Simeon's prophetic words during the temple dedication. He proclaimed God's word and predicted Jesus' ministry. Mary and Joseph had no idea what he was talking about. Mary later pondered his words.

Let's look at Simeon's proclamation of God's word. He addressed the Lord as sovereign. He is the sole ruler of the universe. Just as the Father is King, the son, Jesus Christ, is the exalted one who sits on the eternal throne of David. Jesus fulfills Yahweh's promise to bless all nations through Abraham. That is, all Gentiles, former enemies of Israel, would now be enlightened to see Jesus as their Savior and Lord. The forecasted kingdom of God would include all cultures, tribes and nations. All this is explicit or implied in Simeon's words.

Simeon mentioned a sword. The gospel includes the suffering and death of Mary's baby. It would begin with verbal challenges by teachers and leaders of the temple. Jesus would be rebuked, considered insane and called a blasphemer. He would continually be misunderstood. The final blow, Jesus' death, would include his mother's own suffering. We see a grieving mother standing at the foot of the cross.

The visit by the Magi is part of Simeon's claim that Jesus would be a light to the Gentiles. The Magi "followed" a light in the heavens to find Jesus, the Jewish king. These Persian astrologers exemplify that future non-Jews would come to realize Jesus as the Jewish messiah. They had it partially right. Jesus was king, but not only for the Jewish nation, but for *all* nations. Just as they followed their culture in paying homage to a king with gifts, all future nations would bow at the name of Jesus Christ. Clearly Mary wasn't

CONCLUSION

thinking theologically during this visit. But it *is* important that the church today realize the prophetic significance of the Magi visit.

The untimely escape from Bethlehem to Egypt returning to Nazareth was the fulfillment of specific Old Testament prophecies about messiah. Key to this event are Egypt and Nazareth. Even though each place had a negative memory for Mary and Joseph, ironically each became a place of refuge. Each prophecy has an explicit or implicit messianic reference in the Old Testament.

No Israelite would have had a positive memory of Egypt. Yet the prophet Hosea's "out of Egypt I called my son" is fulfilled when Mary and her family leave Egypt after going there to save Jesus' life. Ironically, Herod helped fulfill Hosea's forecast centuries before. Once again, a promise - fulfillment scenario characterized an event in Mary's young life. Old Testament promises fulfilled in New Testament statements verify biblical truth. Jesus continually mentioned Old Testament texts to validate that he was the fulfillment of the Law and the Prophets.

A second prophecy relates to the fact that Jesus would be called a Nazarene. No explicit words state this as an Old Testament prophecy. It is implied. Matthew simply adds this prophecy to the journey from Egypt to this new obscure village we've earlier discussed. The word for this town has a bitter-sweet connotation. It can suggest *despised* or *branch*. The first notion comes from Isaiah's anticipation of a suffering Savior. The second weaker reference to branch may derive also from Isaiah's mention of messiah as a tender shoot. Jesus returns to his home town of Nazareth and is called Jesus of Nazareth throughout his life.

The church is a third core theological concept emergent from Mary's relationship to Jesus Christ. She urged servants to obey Jesus' words at a wedding reception. When she stood at a door waiting to see her son, Jesus identified motherhood as those who would hear God's word and do God's will. Mary concretely "became a member of the church" at the foot of her son's cross when John took her home as his "new" mother. Finally, when we find Mary praying with her sons and other men and women who cared for her son, we see the church as a community of new mothers and new brothers cutting across traditional religious boundaries about gender. Women and men were sitting together in church. One of those men was Jesus' brother James, the first pastor of the church. James led the early church as a Jewish community of disciples in Jerusalem. He later wrote a letter to Jewish believers scattered around the world. Two of Mary's sons played huge roles in God's mission to save humanity. Jesus as our savior and Lord. James as a pastor and author in the church.

The Apostle Paul defined Jesus' new humanity as a community without gender, ethnic and socio-economic boundaries. He said, "There is neither Jew nor Greek, slave nor free, male nor female, for you are all one in Christ." This is a huge concept of the church which transcends popular notions of inclusion and diversity. Those politically-correct thoughts derive from the Christian church. It's important not to take credit for what started with God. Today's church need not accommodate culture. Jesus was talking about inclusion and diversity long before politicians and pundits. So obedience, grace and the church derive from the incarnation.

Mary Gave God a Body is about the incarnation. The incarnation implies that Jesus is both the message and the medium in one person. Jesus is God in human clothing. He is the convergence of history and God. Mary's baby Jesus is the Christ of history and the Jesus of faith. The incarnation of Jesus Christ as one person with two natures ends the search for the so-called historical Jesus by finding the Christ faith; he is both. He is Jesus of Nazareth. He is Jesus the Christ. He was the second person of the trinity in human form. The incarnation is enriched by the unlikeliness of God's method for coming into the world. A humble obedient teenage woman became God's mother. The Apostle Paul reminds us that it was in weakness that a crucified Christ has saved us on a cross. The key teaching of a crucified Christ has its origin in a helpless infant-God. The historic Jesus of Nazareth is simultaneously the Christ of faith. A church council over fifteen hundred years ago decided that Jesus was one person with two natures: historic and supernatural. In sum, the incarnation is upheld by two distinct pillars: the Holy Mary's virginal conception and the power of the Holy Spirit.

CONCLUSION

The incarnation anticipates the theology of the Holy Spirit. Mary was the first human being to be filled with the Holy Spirit. Her cousin Elizabeth would be next. When Jesus breathed the Holy Spirit into his disciples on resurrection evening, they were filled with the Holy Spirit. Pentecost is the giving of the Holy Spirit to the entire church. Mary was a forerunner to every Christian whose body would be the temple of God. Mary's body was a tabernacle of God, for the glory of God overshadowed her just like the Holy Spirit came over the tabernacle in the desert. When the Word became flesh we need to imagine God hammering stakes for his tent in our campground. That's what John meant when he said that the Word who became flesh "dwelt among us."

The incarnation lays the ground work for the sacraments. A sacrament is an ordinary thing assigned sacred value. Eucharistic bread and wine are ordinary staples of life before they arrive on the Lord's Table. Their rightful place on the table goes back to the incarnation because an ordinary woman became the mother of God. We worship her son who was an ordinary carpenter from Nazareth as the God-human. The cross was a Roman tool of torture before it became the most ubiquitous symbol of Christianity. All sacramental theology derives from the incarnation.

The Christian concept of incarnation distinguishes it from all other world religions. Muhammad is not God incarnate but merely a depository of a message. Islam claims that he was only a messenger, a prophet. Gabriel was a messenger too; but Christianity doesn't worship an angel. Buddhism, on the other hand, speaks of endless incarnations of the transcendental Buddha all of whom die and enter Nirvana. Each is replaced by a new incarnation. The sacred literature of Hinduism asserts a Krishna who repeatedly appears on earth to guide Aryana in the ways of Brahma. Krishna is ahistorical. No credible data exists speaking of Krishna as a god on earth. Hinduism speaks of reincarnation without incarnation of any of its millions of gods. Christianity's historical verification, finality, and irreversibility are evidenced by God who became human once and for all. This historic event has had cosmic and universal implications as modeled by a multi-lingual, cross-cultural church. A major tenet of Christian faith is that such a church will stand hand in hand for eternity praising a wounded lamb who forgives sin and sinners.

As Dietrich Bonhoeffer stated throughout his writings: "Christ exists *as* the church." Note that this statement does not say, "Christ exists *in* the church." When doing theology, it's often the little words that are important. Were Christ merely *in* the church this would imply that other forces exist in the church which are not Christ. This is impossible. Rather Christ equals the church; the church is the same *as* Christ. The key is the word *body*. When the Apostle Paul uses the metaphor *body of Christ* for the church, he is equating a community of believers with Jesus Christ himself. Because Jesus of Nazareth had a physical body, Christ's church has a spiritual body. The incarnation proposes a concrete manifestation of God himself on earth. That's why the church, as his body, is a historic and concrete representation of Christ. The first Christ-followers were able to see, hear, and touch Jesus of Nazareth. Twenty-first century people need to see, hear, and touch God as they come in contact with the church, the body of Christ. When we do, we experience Christ.

God must have been delighted when Gabriel returned with the good news that a poor young teenage woman from Galilee said yes. The rest is history.

Bibliography

Adela, Mother SCTJM, "The Word Became Flesh in Mary's Womb by the Power of the Holy Spirit," pierced hearts.Org/Mother_Adela_hs.html., 2008.
Arndt, William F., and Gingrich, F. Wilbur, *A Greek-English Lexicon of the New Testament,* Chicago: The University of Chicago Press, 1973.
Barker, Kenneth, ed., *The NIV Study Bible*, Grand Rapids: Zondervan, 1985.
Braaten, Carl A. and Robert W. Jenson, *Mary Mother of God,* Grand Rapids: Eerdmans, 2004.
Bischoff, Paul O., *The Human Church*, Eugene, Oregon: Wipf & Stock, 2018.
Bluemel, Craig, "How God Conceived Jesus in Mary's Womb," bibleanswerstand.org/html.
Bonhoeffer, Dietrich, *Christ the Center*, trans., E. H. Robertson, New York: HarperCollins, 1978.
Brown, Raymond E., Karl P. Donfield, Joseph A. Fitzmeyer and John Reumann, *Mary in the New Testament*, New York: Paulist, 1978.
Douglas, J. D., ed., *The New Greek-English Interlinear New Testament*, Wheaton: Tyndale, 1990.
Dupuis, J., "The Uniqueness of Jesus Christ in the Early Christian Tradition," *Religious Pluralism*, Jeevadhara 47 (1978), 406–407.
Edersheim, Alfred, *The Life and Times of Jesus The Messiah*, Volume 1, Peabody, Massachusetts: Hendrickson, 2000.
Gambero, Luigi, *Mary and the Fathers of the Church*, San Francisco: Ignatius, 1999.
Grimes, Nikki, *Portrait of Mary*, New York: Harcourt Brace, 1994.
Kittel, Gerhard, and Geoffrey W. Bromiley, eds., *Theological Dictionary of the New Testament,* Grand Rapids: Eerdmans, 1964.
Moyer, Ginny K., *Mary and Me*, Cincinnati: St. Anthony Messenger, 2008.
Leith, John H., ed., *Creeds of the Churches*, 3rd. edition, Louisville: John Knox, 1982.
Lowry, Mark, *Mary Did You Know?*, Nashville: Thomas Nelson, 1998.
Luedemann, Gerd, *Virgin Birth: The Real Story of Mary and Her Son Jesus*, Harrisburg, Pennsylvania: Trinity International, 1997.

BIBLIOGRAPHY

Mathewes-Green, Frederica, *Mary as the Early Christians Knew Her,* Brewster, Massachusetts: Paraclete, 2007.

May, Herbert G., and Bruce W. Metzger, eds., *The New Oxford Annotated Bible,* New York: Oxford University Press, 1962.

McKnight, Scott, *The Real Mary,* Brewster, Massachusetts: Paraclete, 2007.

Mish, Frederick C., ed. *Merriam-Webster's Collegiate Dictionary Tenth Edition,* Springfield, Massachusetts: Merriam-Webster, Inc., 2002.

Paulus, Johannes PP.II, *Redemptoris Mater,* w2.vatican.va/enc./redemptoris mater.html, 1987.

Pelikan, Jaroslav, *Mary Through the Centuries,* New Haven: Yale University Press, 1996.

Reiss, Jana, ed., *Dietrich Bonhoeffer: God Is in the Manger,* Louisville: John Knox, 2012.

Roberston, Edwin, *Dietrich Bonhoeffer's Christmas Sermons,* ed., Grand Rapids: Zondervan. 2005.

Roten, Johann G., "The Twofold Incarnation," *Marian Library Studies*: Vol. 30, Article 30, (2012) 3–27.

Slick, Matt, "Did God Place Jesus as a Fetus in Mary's Womb?" CARM, https://carm.org.

Warren, Tish Harrison, *Liturgy of the Ordinary,* Downers Grove: InterVarsity, 2016.

Weber, Manfred, ed., *The Mystery of Holy Night,* New York: Crossroad, 1997.

Whitson, William, *The Complete Works of Flavius Josephus,* Green Forest, Arizona: Master and Attic Books, 2010.

www.ingramcontent.com/pod-product-compliance
Lightning Source LLC
Chambersburg PA
CBHW071200090426
42736CB00012B/2397